I0463502

Experiments in She-ness: women and undependent cinema

Experiments in Cinema
yearbook 2016

Edited by Bryan Konefsky with
River Quane, David Camarena and
Angela Beauchamp

A Basement Films Production

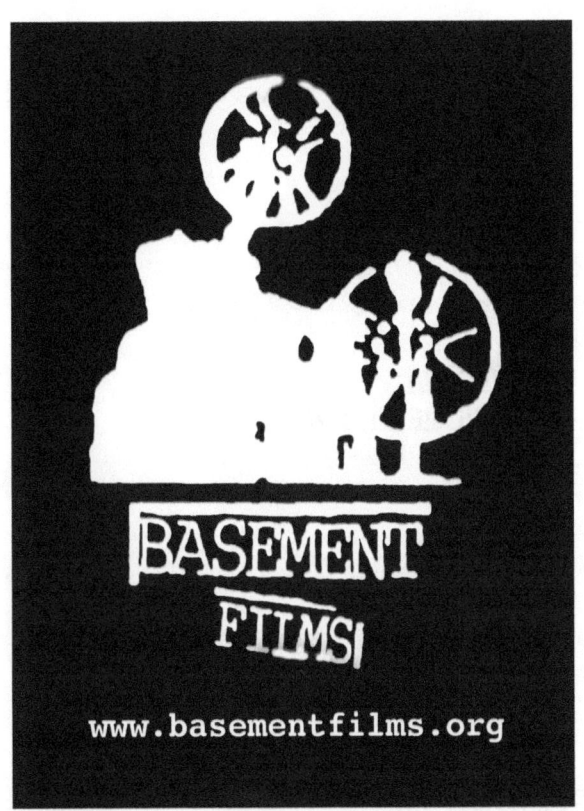

www.basementfilms.org

Experiments in She-ness: women and undependent cinema
Experiments in Cinema
yearbook 2016

Publisher
Basement Films

Editors
Bryan Konefsky, David Camarena, and Angela Beauchamp

Publication Designer
River Quane

Additional Brainstorming

Michelle Mellor and Beth Hansen

Print Run
150

Basement Films
PO Box 9229
Albuquerque, New Mexico
USA 87119
www.basementfilms.org
www.experimentsincinema.org
basementfilms.av@gmail.com

Cover Designer
Beth Hansen

© 2016 Basement Films. All rights reserved.
ISBN 978-1-329-98131-7

Table of Contents

Acknowledgements:

Last year, to celebrate the tenth anniversary of Experiments in Cinema, we published our first yearbook titled *Undependently Yours: Imagining A World Beyond The Red Carpet.* Publishing the text was a remarkable experience thanks in large part to editors River Quane and David Camarena. I never would have imagined publishing a second yearbook, but here we are, one year later, with a new book. Will this now become an annual activity for Experiments in Cinema?

I would like to take this opportunity to thank those who instigated this second yearbook as well as those who were responsible for its realization.

At our festival in 2015, artist in residence Caryn Cline talked about the cultural differences between the terms seminal and ovular. To this end, Caryn threatened to put a posse together and curate an ovular film program for our 2016 event (which she did!). During her residency, Caryn also commented about how Experiments in Cinema provides opportunities for women that many other festivals overlook (thanks, Caryn).

Shortly after the conclusion of our 2015 festival, I received a call from someone named Ariel Dougherty who inquired about using some of the Basement Films 16mm equipment to screen a film from her archive. I didn't realize it at the time, but this was THE Ariel Dougherty who cofounded Women Make Movies! I was star-struck and immediately contacted Experiments in Cinema's Technical Director Michelle Mellor, suggesting that the happenstance of Caryn's earlier "ovular proposal" and my conversation with Ariel about the (her)story of Women Make Movies were signs that we simply must have a women's focus for our 2016 festival. Additionally, it felt obvious that we publish a yearbook mirroring that same theme. I don't think I was able to finish my thoughts before Michelle enthusiastically exclaimed YES!

The Basement Films membership is composed of a group of strong feminist voices, all of whom echoed Michelle's enthusiasm and helped create the impetus necessary for our "she-ness" focus to happen. These strong feminist voices include Beth Hansen (BF Vice President and EIC Workshop Coordinator), Michelle Mellor (BF Community Outreach Coordinator and EIC Technical Director), Senaida Garcia (BF Executive Director), Sahra Saedi (BF Board of Advisors and EIC Hospitality Coordinator), Britney King (BF Board of Directors and EIC Regional Youth Program Coordinator), Peter Lisignoli (BF Board of Directors), and Nicole Hoch (BF member and EIC Print Traffic Controller).

Good ideas are great, but will remain locked in idea-limbo without the hard and careful work it takes to bring them forth into the world. I want to thank our editors, Basement Films members (and more strong feminist voices) David Camarena and River Quane. Additionally, we have brought "on board" Basement Films friend and new yearbook editor Angie Beauchamp, who is coincidentally also teaching an "Images of Women" course in the Department of Cinematic Arts at the University of New Mexico.

Our yearbook would not be possible without all the great contributors whose artwork and words study, explore, expand, and problematize "she-ness." Thanks also to our 2016 artist in residence Kamila Kuc for all her early suggestions as we developed ideas around this yearbook and for her inclusion of Laura Mulvey in her text and in our programming!

Cinematically yours,
Bryan Konefsky
El Presidente, Basement Films
Founder/Director, Experiments in Cinema

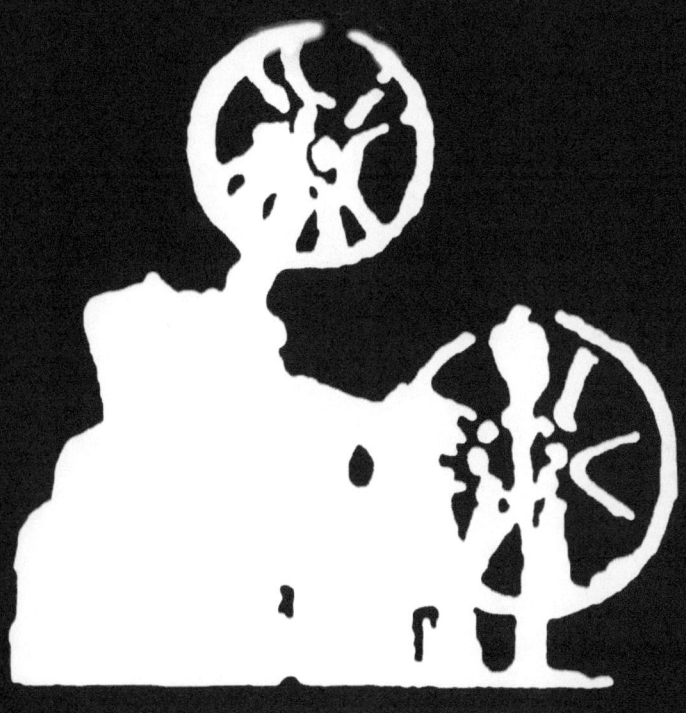

BASEMENT

FILMS

www.basementfilms.org

Introduction
Caryn Cline

This is how it should be done:
Lodge yourself on a stratum, experiment with the opportunities it offers,
find an advantageous place on it,
find potential movements of deterritorialization, possible lines of flight,
experience them, produce flow conjunctions here and there,
try out continuums of intensities segment by segment,
have a small plot of new land at all times.

—Deleuze and Guattari, *A Thousand Plateaus*

It was probably my friend, mentor, and teacher Jeanne Liotta who first told me about Experiments in Cinema. I screened my botanicollage film "In the Conservatory" here in 2011. Later that same year, I attended the Independent Imaging Retreat (the "Film Farm") in Ontario. 2011 was a watershed year for me and my filmmaking practice. Finding these two institutions (or perhaps they found me), I discovered my filmmaking community. I lodge myself on a stratum: I participate in and help sustain an artistic milieu where these organizations live and thrive.

Last year, I wrote an essay for the first edition of the EIC yearbook. I noted the welcome (and unusual) presence of young women as an integral part of the team running the festival. EIC is an *inherently feminist* organization, I claimed. That observation and my Basement Films found footage piece "An Ovular Film" presented at last year's festival led to this gig, writing the introduction to the second edition of the EIC yearbook, *Experiments in She-ness: Women and Undependent Cinema.*

Introduction

In this edition, writer/filmmakers lay out the stakes for us as we experience, shape, document, screen, and live a fourth wave of "experiments in she-ness." They remind us that we need writers as well as filmmakers to tell our stories. A knowledge of our history is crucial, as many contributors witness in their essays. Ours is a history full of gaps, unknown or unacknowledged contributions, and chance inspirations. It is a history made with bedsheets and portable projectors, borrowed equipment, and found footage. It is theory and practice, everyday experiences and memories. It is hand-processed. It is mentorship, training, "each one, teach one." As kerrie welsh notes in "This Precious Authorship," ". . . personal storytelling is capable of inflecting our cultural memory, producing new authors, new histories, and new stories."

"What makes Experiments in Cinema such a great festival?" I asked in my essay last year. I provided some answers, but the truths of this festival's relevance and impact are much deeper than I can begin to articulate. They have to do with the history of this place, with the story of the festival's progenitors, with the personalities, energy, ideas, and media the festival attracts and nurtures. With "Experiments in She-ness," the festival adds another dimension to our understanding of who we are, how far we have come, and what directions we want to travel. At once a legacy and a template, Experiments in Cinema will continue to foster filmmakers who ask new questions and take us to new places.

Feminist Film, A "First Foray" as Change Agent
Ariel Dougherty

"Seeing comes before words" – John Berger, *Ways of Seeing*[1]

"Arm yourself with information, and then challenge that too."
– Chloé Zhao, filmmaker[23]

The spark that ignited one of the most historically significant and socially altering moments of the Women's Liberation Movement (WLM) was an impromptu screening of the film *Schmeerguntz*, the first 16mm film by Gunvor Nelson and Dorothy Wiley made in 1965. Carol Hanisch has long acknowledged the film as being the kernel that crystalized the idea for the Miss America Pageant protest of September 7, 1968.[4] As a filmmaker, here I dive deeper into context, moment, agent, and circuitous accident that ushered this monumental break forward for womankind.[5]

Film can be mind altering. The conditions in which a film is presented also reflect deeply upon one's inner consciousness. The constructs of images one accumulates over time in daily life—especially as dictated by the mainstream, corporate, dominant media—are thereby disrupted by the images of a divergent film. Especially when the circumstances of the film

---

[1] John Berger, *Ways of Seeing* (London: British Broadcasting, 1973).

[22]

[3] "Chloé Zhao," *Filmmaker Magazine*, 2013, http://filmmakermagazine.com/people/chloe-zhao/#.Vij-CmSrTu0.

[4] Carol Hanisch, "What Can Be Learned: A Critique of the Miss America Protest," *Writings by Carol Hanisch*, November 27, 1968, http://carolhanisch.org/CHwritings/MissACritique.html.

[5] This is part of the first chapter of a book Dougherty is writing, *Feminist Filming within Communities*.

screening are unique and or out of the ordinary, that disruption or presentation of images can register a crack or impression in the mind that alters thinking from the status quo. Such a sparkling new view stands in sharp contrast to the daily, more "normal images" one is accustomed to accepting as the reflection of a so-called everyday reality. A cultural shift is in the making.

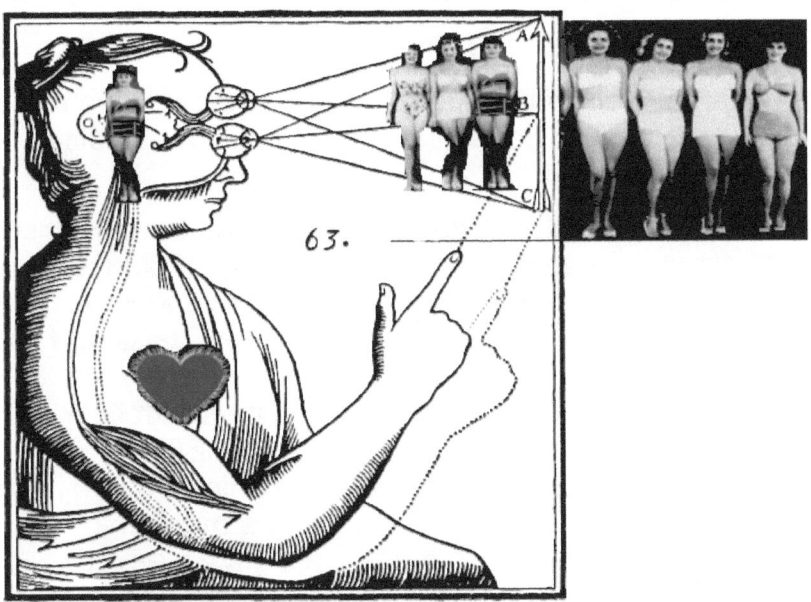

Ariel Dougherty composite image combining *Schmeerguntz* still with Decartes' drawing of Mind/Body Dualism

In a world where the almost totality of filmic images are the constructs of white male thinking, power relationships, dominant understandings, male interactions, and masculine fantasies to see any views of women by women is radical and radicalizing; more so when the views are from women of color.

So this must have been a part of the condition in which Carol Hanisch saw *Schmeerguntz* that summer night in 1968. Since reading Alice Echols' *Daring to Be Bad* and Carol Giardina's *Freedom for Women* and (re)learning that *Schmeerguntz* had stimulated this protest, I have pondered the possibilities of how

Feminist Film, A "First Foray" as Change Agent
this film came to be viewed. Surely as a 15-minute film collage, it was not playing at the local movie theater. Had Hanisch, possibly with a small group of her radical sisters in New York City, gone off to an experimental film screening, like at Film-Makers' Cinematheque? Just how had she seen such a film not readily available in mainstream film venues?

The Illuminating Moment When *Schmeerguntz* Is Screened

Schmeerguntz was not seen by Hanisch alone or with a small cadre of her radical women friends in any standard kind of film screening theater. The screening itself was unique, radical, and, indeed, impromptu.

Clouds of cigarette smoke lingered in the air as Carol Hanisch began to dump the ashtrays after the meeting on a June night in 1968. Almost everyone smoked, and smoked heavily, in the late 1960s. Cigarette butts accumulated in both glass and tin ashtrays after a three-hour meeting. With dozens of women present, the receptacles filled up quickly. The fourth floor office of Southern Conference Educational Fund (SCEF), on Broadway just a few short blocks south of Union Square, was where Hanisch worked. She had secured permission for an embryonic group of women to meet one night a week to discuss their common issues of women's oppression. Coming from different branches of 1960s social political activism—the Civil Rights Movement, the anti-war movement, and the free-speech movement—anywhere from 20 to 50 women showed up weekly. They called themselves New York Radical Women (NYRW). Over the next several years, these women—trailblazers, activists, leaders, and agitators—would branch out into many different groups spearheading and sustaining the largest social movement and societal change in United States history.

Many of these women had participated in the Jeanette Rankin Brigade, a women's action of 5000 within the anti-war demonstration in Washington in January, just five months earlier.[6] This action, which included the Burial of Traditional Womanhood, crystalized divergent, yet rapidly growing women's positions within the larger left movement. Emboldened, the New York women returned back to their city to deepen examination of women's oppression and their pro-women position. Throughout the spring of 1968, NYRW experimented with a new form of discussion and collective awareness. Based on the Chinese Revolution of speaking "bitterness," criticism/self-criticism methods, and Student Non-Violent Coordinating Committee processes of "testifying" about racism, these women worked to craft a way for women to tell and share their experiences with one another and build theory and action from those discussions. Consciousness Raising, or CR as it became known, "the key to building the Women's Liberation Movement"[7] as Carol Hanisch would later describe, was ideal for women. It radicalized women as they discovered deep common experiences among themselves, which overflowed from wellsprings of internalized knowledge and learning based on women's innate intelligence, for which at the time no literature existed, and few words. It was a time of invention and intervention.

These consciousness raising sessions that NYRW devised as tools for deepening self-awareness from women's personal experiences stimulated both excitement and anxiety. Maybe that caused the women to puff on cigarettes more rapidly, piling up the butts. Especially in the heat of this June night, Hanisch was reluctant to shut the large windows. The outside air, hot though it was, provided the only relief from the stuffy smoked filled room. A particular series of images from the film that someone had brought to the meeting darted in Hanisch's mind, as the smoke lingered in the air. Women in their bathing suits at

---

[6] The Community Newsreel's film on this march, *Jeanette Rankin Brigade* (8m, B&W, 1968), is often considered the "first" film that speaks about the emerging women's liberation movement. (They claim 10,000 women were there.)
[7] Carol Hanisch, Speech at Marist College, "Women and Society Conference," June 11, 1999.

the Miss America contest and the role the contest had in shaping women's sense of themselves tapped powerful memories in Carol.

Schmeerguntz slipped through the gate of the projector for only fifteen short minutes, dancing its fused images before the hungry eyes of women deprived of stories about their own real lives. In the modestly sized office, crowded with some twenty women, the film was screened onto a wall. The whirr of the projector clashed with the voice-overs, music, and sound effects. The vast majority of collaged images never registered with Hanisch. The bathing beauty scenes at the Miss America Pageant were what imprinted into her consciousness in a new kind of way. Over forty years ago in a critique of the Miss America action Hanisch wrote: "The movie had flashes of the Miss America contest in it. I found myself sitting there remembering how I had felt at home with my family watching the pageant as a child, an adolescent, and a college student. I knew it had evoked powerful feelings."[8]

In our email exchange, Hanisch recounts: "I barely remember it, only that I wasn't particularly thrilled with the film itself. Too artsy or something and maybe it went over my head. It was just the women in the bathing suit competition that sparked the protest idea."[9] I pressed to know more. Did SCEF have their own projector? No, Hanisch flatly responded. This then demanded considerable commitment on the part of the person who brought the film. The bearer of the film also had to lug a 16mm projector to the meeting. After thousands of community screenings, I have a strong perspective on the degree of energy involved in presenting a film, especially a short one, in such a circumstance. At the time, 16mm projectors, bulky at about 1 foot by 16" by 24," were built nonetheless to be portable. Solid workhorses, they were relatively available in schools, libraries, and in some community groups. Our resourceful activist knew how to get her hands on one. They were a hefty carry at about 35 pounds, especially via subway.

---

[8] Carol Hanisch, "What Can Be Learned."
[9] Carol Hanisch, Message to the author, April 20, 2015, e-mail.

Ariel Dougherty

When it became clear that Hanisch herself had not arranged for the showing of the film, eagerly I asked, "Who did?" Recollections over time wander or fade altogether. Hanisch was clear, explanatory: "I don't recall who brought the film and projector. It was not the type of thing we did at our meetings. We were not very formally organized so someone probably just showed up with it."[10]

Carol Hanisch's response dramatically painted the screening as informal, in fact affirmatively *impromptu*. As of this writing, an unidentified woman was the presenter and projectionist—really the *agent provocateur*. Since my first inquires of Hanisch about the circumstances, I have now spoken with eight other women who might have been present that night.[11] Some have stated they were away. If one had been present, she doesn't remember the screening of the film, let alone who might have brought it to the NYRW meeting.

Locating a projector was one thing; having a print of the California made and distributed *Schmeerguntz* in New York City in the early summer of 1968 was another. My filmmaker on-the-ground experience of NYC in the period points to barely a half a dozen possibilities. This detective work is still ongoing.

---

[10] Ibid.

[11] Bev Grant and Robin Morgan both responded via emails that they don't remember seeing the film. Kathie Sarachild via email said she was away in Southern California in the early summer of 1968 but was back in NYC by time of the meeting at Sandy Springs, MD. Via Facebook messages, Peggy Dobbins reported she was in Colorado and didn't return until the planning for the protest was under way. Neither Judith Weston (aka Judith Garret) nor Rivka Polatnick had any memories on the film. When I had dinner with Roslyn Baxandall on April 26, 2015, she didn't recall the film screening, but she was present for the final planning of the protest. Extensive notes of the details of the mechanics for the protest exist in the Robin Morgan papers at Duke University including the letters to and from the Mayor of Atlantic City and the legal action attempting to stop the protest.

Feminist Film, A "First Foray" as Change Agent
By the time Hanisch closed the windows, finished cleaning up, and locked the SCEF office door behind her that June night, she reminisced: "I didn't immediately propose the Miss America protest idea. I wasn't sure our new Movement was large enough to be able to carry it off yet. It ruminated in my mind."[12]

From the Kitchen Sink: The Making of *Schmeerguntz*

Three years before the impromptu screening at New York Radical Women, Dorothy Wiley and Gunvor Nelson, two housewife/artists, were amassing footage to shape an untold story onto celluloid. It was about the small things in their everyday lives. Working purely from their intuitions, they were collecting material through their homegrown film skills *and* as time from raising their children allowed: "With *Schmeerguntz* we wanted to make a 16mm movie. But we had no subject. Then, one day I was looking at all the gunk in the sink and thought of the contrast between what we do, and what we see that we 'should' be—in ads and things—and that was the idea right from there, the sink."[13]

Sink gunk had inspired the film! We are definitely not illuminating a Doris Day-Rock Hudson Hollywood feature here. The quote is from an enlightening, matter-of-fact interview Brenda Richardson conducted with both the filmmakers for *Film Quarterly* in 1971. Richardson opened her now germinal interview by stating that the two women "have been friends for eleven years." Dorothy went on to describe how they worked together: "We always divided it up equally for some reason. We both filmed, we both edited, and we seemed to agree on things."

Richardson then asked the filmmakers, "What do you think the advantages are of making movies together?" Wiley answered first: "I was never highly motivated to do something for myself.

---

[12] Hanisch, Message to the author.

[13] Brenda Richardson, "Women, Wives, Film-Makers: An Interview with Gunvor Nelson and Dorothy Wiley." *Film Quarterly* 25.1 (Autumn 1971), 35.

10

But if I said to Gunvor I'd be there at eleven, to please her I'd be there at eleven, and do it. But if it had been up to me, I would probably have done more dishes or something." Then Nelson: "Yes, for me too. It's like getting away from the fear of it or something."[14]

The collaboration clearly strengthened their joint resolve, spurred them on in their commitment to the project, and eliminated the fear of tackling something unknown. Especially for this film, they were supporting one another in learning the craft of filmmaking. Prior to *Schmeerguntz* neither had 16mm

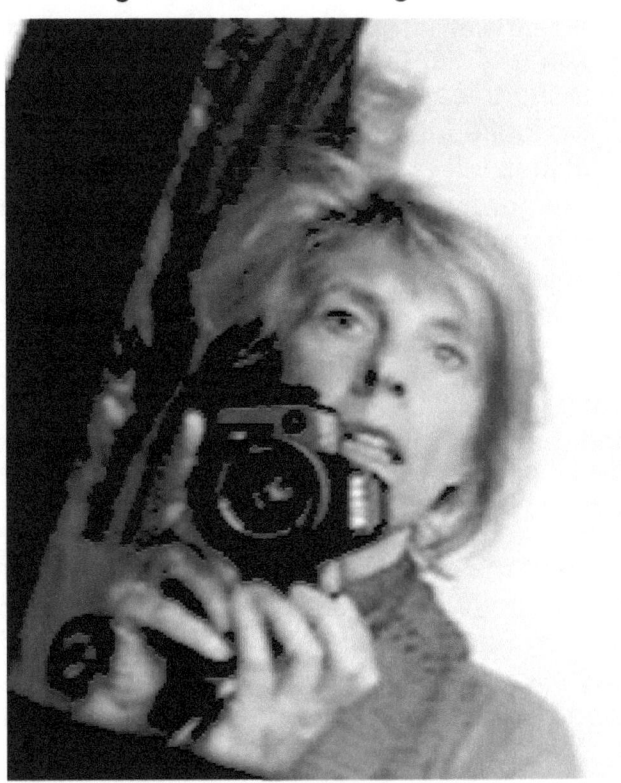

film experience. Both of their husbands were experimental filmmakers just starting out their own careers. Wiley: "I can remember telling Bob [Nelson], we wanted to make a movie and he just sat down and in half an hour he showed us how to

---

[14] Ibid.

use a camera, and that you could move stuff around, and that was all the instruction we ever had."[15]

That 30-minute lesson was their entire schooling. Inventiveness and ingenuity were the rule of the day. In program notes for a 1992 screening of *Schmeerguntz* at the San Francisco Cinematheque, Wiley described more about how they went about filming various sequences:

> Our footage and sound of the Miss America contest was filmed right off the TV in 1965. We had a neighbor that wasn't the best housekeeper, and we asked to film at her house to illustrate some of our points. I know that when we were trying to capture some of the crudeness of life and we looked thru the camera at, say, piles of dirty dishes left on the table till the next day, or a filthy refrigerator, what we saw in the camera was ethereally beautiful, the light would illuminate objects as if we were in heaven, and we fell in love with film.[16]

Wiley: "...the soundtrack, we didn't know how that would fit in until we saw the copy of it. Nelson: "Like when you threw up, and 'he kissed her again' is on the soundtrack. We didn't plan that."[17] Nelson: "Film is the one place in my life where I have an illusion of control."[18]

New Year's Eve at the end of 1965 was when Wiley and Nelson screened the film *Schmeerguntz* for an audience for the first time. It was in Sausalito, the Marin County hamlet just across the bay from San Francisco. Five other films played before *Schmeerguntz*, the last film on the program. When it

---

[15] Ibid, 34.

[16] "San Francisco Cinematheque Program Notes." *Internet Archive*, 1992, http://archive.org/stream/sanfranciscocine92sanfrich/sanfrancis cocine92sanfrich_djvu.txt, 87-88.

[17] Richardson, op cit, p 36.

[18] "San Francisco Cinematheque Program Notes," 87-88.

spooled off its reel and threaded through the projector gates to shine its collage of images onto the screen, immediately the audience roared. When it was over, people stood and clapped. Nelson: "Bill Geis came over, and he had never spoken to us as human beings before, and it was as if he was seeing us for the first time...." Wiley: "I remember making that distinction, why did I need to have some kind of product in order to be talked to."[19]

At the 1966 4th Annual Ann Arbor Film Festival, today the longest running independent and experimental festival in North America, *Schmeerguntz* won the top honor. The film went on to win awards at a half dozen other festivals that year.

While Nelson and Wiley definitely were a part of the independent, experimental film scene that had a profound blossoming in and around San Francisco in the 1960s, Gunvor has been especially adamant that she does not see her films as experimental. In fact, she perceives "experimental" as something incomplete, unfinished. Instead, she self-defines her work as "personal film," "since it stems from one person."[20] She believes that if you go deep enough into your being to find the essence, what would evolve out of that experience would be universal. The more personal it is, she believes, the more interesting.[21]

"Woman filmmaker" was not a term that appealed to Wiley and Nelson. They insisted instead that they were artists.

Actualizing the *Schmeerguntz* Image into Action

When Carol Hanisch locked SCEF's office that June evening after the screening of *Schmeerguntz*, she had not yet said a word to anyone about the images that sprouted in her mind. Hanisch believed there were not enough members in the newly

---

[19] Richardson, op cit, p 36.
[20] John Sundholm,"Gunvor Nelson and the Aesthetics of Sensual Materiality," *Avanto Helsinki Media Art Festival*, 167.
[21] Richardson, op cit, p 40.

forming women's liberation movement to carry off an action that began to take hold in her thoughts. All that would change a little over a month later.

At Sandy Springs, Maryland a "score of women" from New York, Chicago, Durham, Baltimore, Boston, and Gainesboro gathered on August 2 to break the isolation of local organizing.[22] This handful of women gathered for three days from separate locales to share what they were doing in terms of women's liberation in their home communities. At the heart of almost every discussion was the central question: "Was the struggle against capitalism or men?" Among the many issues they discussed were their pro-women views, newly evolving consciousness raising, and the inclusion of black women in the larger conference they were organizing for November in Illinois.

Excited about what she had observed, on the drive back to NYC from this planning meeting, Carol Hanisch shared with her sister car travelers Cindy Cisler, Kathie Sarachild, and a few others the scenes that *Schmeerguntz* had etched in her mind. "The Sandy Springs Conference confirmed to me that we were indeed ready."[23]

The very next day after returning from Sandy Springs, Hanisch and Kathie Sarachild borrowed a car and drove to Jones Beach, New York. There looking out over the expanse of the Atlantic Ocean and soaking in its salty spray, the two women sketched out the very first plans for a national women's action to take place at the Miss America Pageant. The heralded national contest of American female beauty was only four weeks away. At the next New York Radical Women's meeting, Hanisch put forth her proposal and sketched out the plans she and Kathie had outlined.[24] The women delved into consciousness raising to explore their own feelings about the

---

[22] Carol Giardina, *Freedom for Women: Forging the Women's Liberation Movement, 1953-1970.* (Gainesville, FL: U of Florida, 2010), 141.

[23] Hanisch, Message to the author.

[24] Carol Hanisch and Kathie Sarachild, Messages to the author, April 21, 2015, e-mail.

pageant and to illicit "a gaggle of ideas" on how to shape the protest.[25] Hanisch underscored: "The Miss America protest was a zap action, as opposed to person to person group action. Zap actions are using our presence as a group and/or media to make women's oppression into a conscious social issue."[26]

From the nascent images captured of the 1965 Miss America Pageant by Nelson and Wiley, Carol Hanisch transformed her own experiences about the beauty contest into a collective force with her sister radicals. A group of twenty or thirty women dreamed up the "Freedom Trash Can" in which non-necessary items would be tossed, plus the crowning of the sheep and the "inside group" to unfurl the banner. They sought the Atlantic City Mayor's permission for their action. Through a leaflet distributed to their networks, they summoned sister activists from other cities, and they issued a press release especially directed at women reporters to join and report the upcoming action. Years later Carol Hanisch concludes her initial email to me: "I remember not being particularly thrilled to give up CR time to watch a film. Fate has its interesting twists and turns!"[27] She recognizes the surprising origins and the irony of her own perspective in the role that *Schmeerguntz*, a film, had on this remarkable, historic protest.

(Un)becoming History

"Be sure to show the film more than once," was how Jeanne Betancourt concluded the write-up about *Schmeerguntz* in her book *Women in Focus*.[28] Written from her experience of showing high school girls women-identified films, it was an early 1970s primer, like today's #HSfeminism on use of films in classrooms. Maybe if this had been done at the NYWR showing of the film in June 1968, more women would

---

[25] Ibid. and Giardina, op cit, p 141.
[26] Carol Hanisch, "What Can Be Learned."
[27] Hanisch, Message to the author.
[28] Jeanne Betancourt, *Women in Focus* (Dayton, OH: Pflaum Pub., 1974), 120.

Feminist Film, A "First Foray" as Change Agent
remember the screening and who brought the film. Had there
been discussion about the film afterwards, and Hanisch had put
forth her idea then, maybe the context of the film screening
would have registered with more women.

Nelson and Wiley struggled against being "pigeonholed" by
insisting they were artists and not solely "woman filmmakers."
Such dichotomy of identification harps at the hearts, and
history, of far too many women. This is an often-repeated
mantra in the present—of many women who believe in all the
attributes of feminism, but refuse to call themselves feminists. A
contradiction, it rings profoundly.

As history now looks back on this period of experimental
filmmaking, a new (*really the same old*) problem arises. The
short of it is The Canon vs. The Other. But even within the
context of histories of The Other, there is yet another "other."
The small case, diminutive "other" is almost always women; the
small "o" harkens back to what the 1960s women filmmakers
were recording of the "little stuff" and the repetition in their own
lives—that which the predominant male culture blindly, often
with hostility, fails to see, understand, appreciate, and
recognize. The harbinger of the all-pervasive mainstream,
patriarchal culture casts a very long, oppressive shadow. For
example, the well-received book *Subject to Change* by Dierdre
Boyle[29] omits any mention of the sixty-plus women's video
groups that existed in communities across the United States in
the 1970s.[30] How does this repeatedly happen?

In March 2015, *Schmeerguntz* was screened at the Irish Film

---

[29] Deirdre Boyle, *Subject to Change: Guerrilla Television
Revisited* (New York: Oxford UP, 1997).

[30] Three pages list feminist film and video groups compiled for
the Conference of Feminist Film and Video Organizations, Jan
30, 1975. Sixty-seven groups are based in the USA; another
eleven groups listed are in the international community. These
lists should be in Women Make Movies organizational papers.
They are in this author's papers at Schlesinger Library:
http://oasis.lib.harvard.edu/oasis/deliver/~sch01216.

Ariel Dougherty

Institute in Dublin, Ireland. In advance of the screening, Alice Butler, the curator of the program, and Daniel Fitzpatrick, another curator with the Experimental Film Club, outlined the problem specifically for Wiley and Nelson. Butler:

> Her [Nelson's] works are very female centric[31] and even though *Schmeerguntz* is a general comment on consumerism and the inherent deceits of advertising and commercial culture, it's very much focused on what that means for women.... Nelson and Wiley didn't see *Schmeerguntz* or the work they did together as forming part of the feminist movement of the time although it undeniably speaks to feminist concerns. Perhaps the issue was that they felt the feminist tag would leave less room for more open interpretations.

Fitzpatrick:

> At the time when she's making work, there are certain stages within that period where situating yourself not only as a feminist filmmaker but even as a woman filmmaker instead of just a filmmaker, is intensely problematic. Arguably it remains problematic and it becomes too easy to be pigeonholed and as it is *she seems to have been unfairly neglected in terms of writings about her work*. In all the canonical writings around experimental & avant-garde film, through that index, she doesn't show up a lot of the time. People know her work but she has a sort of invisibility that I'm sure at some stage she didn't want to further contribute to by allowing herself to

---

[31] "Female-centric" or "women-centric" crop up as terms more and more. I find them difficult and pejorative. It lacks an affirmation that "women-identified" conveys. Further "women-identified" is more historically accurate, referring to the origins of creation of the term and its meaning.

be pigeonholed. [emphasis added]

Butler: "...there has been some considerable recognition of Nelson's work—there was a complete retrospective at MoMA in 2006 for instance but I agree that you would expect her to turn up more in academic reference material." Fitzpatrick: "Even Visionary Film, or any other collected writings about experimental avant-garde film that are contemporary to her time seem to have left her out to some degree."[32]

Slipping on the patriarchal banana-peel of historical record making, women *still* are damned if they do and damned if they don't—and perpetually pigeonholed. Like the imaginative revolutionary film *Schmeerguntz* itself and the dramatic zap action in which a Women's Liberation Movement banner is unfolded on live national television, women again need to shake up the status quo. Such a new film and or zap action needs to unsnarl patriarchy head on. Let us condemn the historical silencing and the constant erasing of women from history. At every turn we must ask, and what about the women? We need to more than peek into women's worlds. It needs a spotlight and red carpet.

It is now two generations later. The permutations and massiveness of today's media, especially corporate media, have even more undue influence. It continues to distort our lives ever more. Data shows, the central behind-the-camera roles for women in Hollywood films leveled off twenty years ago in 1995! Believe me, it had not advanced very far.[33] In a recent news article a mother, Beth Berry, calls out the challenges she faces, listing seventeen myths of mothering she would like to

---

[32] Alice Butler and Daniel Fitzpatrick, "*Schmeerguntz*: Conversation between Daniel Fitzpatrick and Alice Butler," *Experimental Film Club*, http://experimentalfilmclub.blogspot.ie/2015/03/projection-49.html.
[33] Dinah Eng, "Meet the Woman Who Started the EEOC Investigation into Sexism in Hollywood," *Fortune*, Oct. 19, 2015, http://fortune.com/2015/10/19/meet-the-woman-who-started-the-eeoc-investigation-into-sexism-in-hollywood.

see change. Number two mirrors the very same things Nelson and Wiley recorded in 1965:

> ***Life as presented in stores and advertising reflects the way life actually is.*** *A truer story:* The "reality" presented to us as consumers—*that life can or should be perpetually pleasant, tidy, organized, beautiful and—blemish-free*—is a myth of the most seductive sorts. Because we *want* our lives to feel less stressful and more abundant, it's easy to get caught up in retail fairytales, *allowing them to increase the size of our gap.* We'd be wise, however, to consider the greater implications of allowing *any* profit-seeker to shape our sense of prioritization, beauty or truth. I find it helpful to keep the word *fairytale* in mind anytime I enter a shopping center or flip through a magazine.[34] [emphasis added]

It is poetic that flashes within *Schmeerguntz* caught Carol Hanisch's imagination, she who disparaged such a screening that would take away time for more important work of thinking and discussion about conscious raising. That the filmmakers identify their work as "personal cinema" is fortuitous. Only six months after the protest, Carol Hanisch wrote the feminist treatise that has permeated into the dominate culture the most, "The Personal Is Political." In a 2006 reprint of her 1969 essay,[35] she claims that she did not create that title; however, it was an emphatic call for the use of consciousness raising as a political tool for eliciting discussion and knowledge of the issues that were central to women based on their lived experiences.

---

[34] Beth Berry, "17 Modern Myths That Are Making Motherhood Miserable," *Mothering*, Nov. 2, 2015, http://www.mothering.com/articles/17-modern-myths-making-motherhood-miserable.

[35] Carol Hanisch, "The Personal Is Political." *Writings by Carol Hanisch.* 1969 (2006), http://www.carolhanisch.org/CHwritings/PersonalisPol.pdf.

Feminist Film, A "First Foray" as Change Agent

Isn't this after all how Wiley and Nelson see their filmmaking as a way to explore personal experiences to arrive at a universal understanding? On the West Coast women, Nelson lived on a perch above the Pacific Ocean and Wiley, a frequent visitor, lived nearby. In a moment of fervored consciousness, Hanisch and Sarachild escaped New York City to soak in the churning waves of the Atlantic Ocean to flush out the shell of the most strategically significant action, a "first foray" as Hanisch states, of the Women's Liberation Movement.

A phantom of the summer night, the mystery woman, our *agent provocateur*, linked the two groups. She brought the constructed thousands of frames of celluloid crafted by two young women, friends, mothers, who united to tell a novel cinematic story of the minutia in women's lives. While there were perhaps twenty-five women in the room that hot June night, only one caught the juxtaposition of a set of images to envision other possibilities. Dozens of activists shaped the action after its initial framing by Hanisch with Kathie Sarachild. Just a hundred women participated in the action on the boardwalk and inside the pageant hall. The zap action, three years after Wiley and Nelson filmed the 1965 event with their Bolex, brought the Women's Liberation Movement into the nation's living rooms and ignited a full-fledged movement across the globe.

"When Gunvor took out her Bolex camera, the strangest, most intriguing transformations would happen on the screen. Green apples would devour themselves with unfathomable delicacy. Snowstorms would purr like a prowling cat." – Lynne Sachs, student of Gunvor Nelson's at San Francisco Art Institute[36]

Like a prowling cat, film can purr change and in extraordinary, often inexplicable ways. As in this case with *Schmeerguntz*, it

---

[36] Lynne Sachs, "Thoughts on the Films of Gunvor Nelson." *Website of Filmmaker Lynne Sachs*. Nov.-Dec. 2004, http://www.lynnesachs.com/tag/thoughts-on-gunvor-nelson.

can herald a whole movement before an entire nation.[37]

---

[37] *Up Against The Wall Ms. America* is the eight minute
Community Newsreel film that was made about the Miss
America Pageant Protest.

This Precarious Authorship: Some Notes on Home Movies, Homemaking, and Alternative Genealogies

kerrie welsh

I wasn't too good at it. You know, when you have little kids, and you're taking care of them, you have a hard time taking movies too.

~ Helen Baltus Franz (1919-2009)

Start with the screen. *Flickering. Unnatural movement. A young girl in a red coat walks down a dirt road. She must've been my age. Little. My aunts and uncles' laughter. Knees at eye-level.* For years, I thought this memory of a slideshow that moved must have been my imagination. An anachronistic fantasy by a filmmaker in a family crowded around a still, square screen. My maternal grandfather, George Benedict Franz, was a prolific amateur photographer and slide-showman. He developed over 20,000 photographs in a tiny makeshift darkroom below the basement stairs in the Baltimore home where my mother came of age. He made a moon for me there, so I would know that you cannot see the truth: there's only magic.

His parents gave him his first camera, a Kodak Brownie, when he was ten. The legacy of that gift was long lasting: my grandfather took pictures from his boyhood into his eighties. He trained his son Karl in photography and later Karl's son Max. A lineage: from amateur to professional in three generations. Was there also an assumption that men made images and women made homes?

Grandmom had secret spaces too. Her cramped sewing room unfolded magically behind the boys' bedroom in a small converted closet. Spools of thread of every color, collected over years at weekend flea markets; tins of mismatched, misshaped buttons; piles of clothing hanging to hide behind. Grandmom made me shy. Ironing boards swung down, tabletops transformed with the touch of her hand: every corner a miracle. She was a master of machines.

I was already in film school when my uncle David gave out copies of our family's few, long forgotten, home movies as a Christmas gift. Suddenly, the truth of the flickering girl. The heat of the screen. The revelation that my grandmother, Helen Baltus Franz, had shot my family's home movies.

Hearsay, HerStory, and Home Movies

Histories of women and the moving image are constantly being rewritten, revised, and redacted. The exhilarating proliferation of feminist film historiography over the last fifteen years has built upon the work of feminist film theory and the feminist film movement to create a formidable, public body of work that has increased access to what this volume is calling *cinematic she-ness*.[1] In the present moment, definitions of *she-ness* are being radically questioned and redefined legally at the grassroots level and in the mainstream popular consciousness through the work of women such as Laverne Cox, Jill Soloway, and Caitlyn Jenner, among many others. As we take this peek into past, present, and future *she-ness* and cinema, the ACLU and the Equal Employment Opportunity Commission are investigating widespread gender discrimination in the entertainment industries, recalling both the National Organization for Women's lawsuits against the major networks in the 1970s, and the much earlier public protests filmmakers such as Lois Weber articulated against the dwindling opportunities for female directors in the early 1920s.[2] Indeed, the public history of

---

[1] For recent directions in feminist film historiography see: Christine Gledhill and Julia Knight, eds., *Doing Women's Film History: Reframing Cinemas, Past and Future* (Urbana-Champaign: University of Illinois Press, 2015); also see: Shelley Stamp, ed., *Feminist Media Histories* (2015).
[2] kerrie welsh, ed., unpublished oral history with Louise Tiranoff, *Women in the Director's Chair Oral History Project*; see also Allison Perlman, "Feminists In The Wasteland,"

This Precarious Authorship: Some Notes on Home Movies, Homemaking, and Alternative

cinematic she-ness is a fraught one: the era between Lois Weber's pointed protestations and the NOW lawsuits of the Women's Liberation Movement might be called a low-point, or you might just call it Classical Hollywood Cinema. To understand cinematic she-ness in this era one might turn elsewhere.

In this paper, I would like to turn to personal history to ask how it might sustain us in the moments when public discourse lets us down, and how such private histories might also challenge and revise established notions of cinematic she-ness. In turning back to my grandmother's 8mm films produced in the 1940s, I hope we might better understand the politics of authorship, the reiteration of power, and possibilities of creative lineage beyond the traditional frameworks so wrapped up with existing circuits of cultural capital, art markets, academia, and industrial logic. As filmmakers and scholars from Maya Deren and Chantal Akerman to Annette Kuhn and B. Ruby Rich have demonstrated, personal storytelling is capable of inflecting our cultural memory, producing new authors, new histories, and new stories. In culling the experiential and common sense methodologies of my grandmother's life, I desire to create an alternative framework, a lineage that *speaks me* just as clearly as the dominant discourses do not.

After learning that my grandmother had taken our home movies, I asked her if I could interview her about them. She flatly refused. Shortly thereafter, I **surreptitiously** recorded a conversation with her in which I tested her patience by asking her everything I could think of about this subject, which was much more important to me than to her. (My grandmother wasn't a woman who missed much, and I believe that she knew I was recording our conversations despite her refusal, although we never discussed it.) When pressed about her role as the family filmmaker, she told me the following story about one of

---

Feminist Media Studies 7, no. 4 (2007): 413-431; on Lois Weber see Shelley Stamp, *Lois Weber in Early Hollywood* (Berkeley: University of California Press, 2015).

kerrie welsh

their camping trips:

> You ever been to Watkins Glen? Let me tell you:
> one time we were at Watkins Glen. I had two of
> 'em: Linda and Karl. Two and a four year old, and
> here I'm supposed to take pictures. A movie of
> this and watch them too. You know how that
> place is. It's coming down the mountains, there's
> stones and steps, and I think I was on that trail
> about ten minutes when I blew my top. I says, to
> hell with this—I'm going. I grabbed both of 'em by
> the hand and said I'm going back to camp. You
> can have this place! So I think that was the end of
> my movie-taking.

She laughed, telling me how she made harnesses for my mom
and Uncle Karl back at camp so she could hold on to them.
Then she told me the story again through her laughter:

> He was taking pictures and his father was taking
> pictures, and I was supposed to take moving
> pictures. And I says, this is too much. I can't stand
> this! So I grabbed the kids and I went back to
> camp where it was nice and flat and they could
> just play. That was the end of that.

My grandmother's double refusal of this precarious authorship
was adamant, and yet, it was not the end of that. The movies
she took extend over approximately another ten years.

Her desire to refuse authorship of the family films is shared with
my grandfather. According to my mother, the movie camera
was a wedding gift from my grandfather's brother Larry, who
was the real auteur of the family. As my grandmother told me,
"Uncle Larry used to take movies a lot. He took some of us.
Grandpop lost interest right away. He didn't want any parts of
'em." It seems that taking the home movies was passed off to
my grandmother as an essential piece of homemaking, another

This Precarious Authorship: Some Notes on Home Movies,
Homemaking, and Alternative
part of the duty of being a good mother.[3]

Homemaking Movies: Mechanical Memories and Home Economics

If you can thread a sewing machine, you can thread a projector, and if you can follow a recipe, you can do still photography developing.

~ Liane Burton, 1972[4]

The period during which my grandmother took home movies in the 1940s and early 1950s is generally considered a period of patriarchal familialism. As Roger Odin has recently described it, "Within this structure the father has a particular position; it is he who directs the formation of familial memory," and "obviously, it is he who shoots the films."[5] My grandmother's attitude toward her films clearly negotiates this familial space, taking up the camera as a duty of motherhood under the direction or encouragement of my grandfather. What then, can my grandmother's footage show us in relation to what Marianne Hirsch calls the familial gaze? How does my grandmother's footage compare to that shot by the more traditional "daddy-

---

[3] On mothers as the guardians of memory, see Patricia Holland, "History, Memory and the Family Album," cited in Richard Fung, "Remaking Home Movies," in *Mining the Home Movie: Excavations in Histories and Memories*, eds., Karen L. Ishizuka and Patricia R. Zimmermann (University of California Press, 2007), 31, 40.

[4] Quoted in Paula Rabinowitz, "Medium Uncool: Women Shoot Back; Feminism, Film and 1968—A Curious Documentary," *Science & Society* 65, no. 1 (2001): 93.

[5] Roger Odin, "The Home Movie and Space of Communication," in *Amateur Filmmaking: The Home Movie, the Archive, the Web*, eds. Laura Rascaroli, Gwenda Young, Barry Monahan (New York: Bloomsbury Academic, 2014).

filmer" critiqued by feminist filmmakers and scholars such as Michelle Citron and Patricia Erens?[6] As new archival evidence begins to suggest that more mothers shot the family films than previously assumed, how might my grandmother's footage compare to other homemaking filmmakers of her generation?[7]

Scholarly work on the home movie has tended to use the touchstones of advertising and instruction manuals, cine-clubs, commercial cinema, and/or the avant-garde to make sense of these commonplace visual objects. None of these contexts speak to my grandmother's production. The camera was a gift received as a burden, so reading her films in relation to advertisements and manuals would misread them. While she did describe enjoying musicals and serials, she was not an avid film fan, and film going was not a big part of the family culture or her home movie *oeuvre*. Although she was engaged with crafts and design, particularly sewing, her films have no artistic pretentions: these are not the works of what Charles Tepperman calls "serious amateurs," whose work requires further attention than the "simplicity" of home movies.[8] Rather, my grandmother's films are best understood in relation to the labor of mothering and *homemaking*.

My grandmother was actively involved with the Overlea Homemakers, one of Maryland's 400 plus extension homemakers clubs. This nationwide network of clubs was created in 1914 by an act of Congress, which "created

---

[6] See the special issue on home movies of *The Journal of Film and Video 38*, nos. 3-4 (1986). Fred Camper's classic "Some Notes on the Home Movie" points out that feminists have "noted the ways in which little girls are encouraged to look pretty for the eyes/lens of daddy-filmer."

[7] See for example: Jeffrey Rouff cited in Karan Sheldon, "Home Movies," *Northeast Historic Film*, Accessed December 30, 2015: http://oldfilm.org/content/home-movies.

[8] Charles Tepperman, *Amateur Cinema: The Rise of North American Moviemaking, 1923-1960* (Berkeley: University of California Press, 2014), 6.

cooperative extension services at the nation's land-grant universities, including the University of Maryland."[9] During this period in the early and middle-twentieth century, homemaking was being imagined as a scientific pursuit, and the 1914 *bill inaugurating the extension homemaker's program suggests that "there is no more important work in the country" than home management.*[10] The mechanical memories my grandmother produced might be best understood as an extension of the new scientific and civic advances in home economics. While my research is still at a preliminary stage, I'd like to suggest that considering the homemakers clubs in relation to progressive politics, class mobility, and collective identity might complicate and enrich our understanding of home movies and mid-century American cinematic she-ness more broadly. The model of *The Homemakers* is distinct from that of the isolated upper middle class *housewife* later critiqued by Betty Friedan and the Women's Liberation Movement. This alternative model of collective identification supported by government funding offers a forgotten framework for understanding my grandmother's films, and perhaps more broadly, *homemaking movies* as a genre distinct from the masculine identified "home movies" studied by scholars such as Odin.

Paula Rabinowitz has argued that before the Women's

---

[9] Brendan Kirby, "Homemakers Clubs Change Focus over 80 Years," *Herald Mail Media*, Dec. 26, 1997, http://articles.herald-mail.com/1997-12-26/news/25108806_1_homemakers-clubs-county-women-cooking-and-canning, and Karen Overstreet, "Extension Homemakers Become Community Leaders," *LSU Ag Center, Louisiana Agriculture Magazine*, Spring 2014, *https://www.lsuagcenter.com/en/communications/publications/a gmag/Archive/2014/Spring/ExtensionHomemakersbecomecom munityleaders.htm.*

[10] Helen Sheppard, quoted in Karen Gardner, "Walkersville Homemakers Club In Md. To Disband," *CBS Baltimore*, Jan. 26, 2012, http://baltimore.cbslocal.com/2012/01/26/walkersville-homemakers-club-in-md-to-disband.

Liberation Movement, "underground cinematic revisions of home movies" by filmmakers such as Naomi Levine, Storme De Hirsch, and Barbara Rubin "paved the way for a new radical feminist cinema, even for radical feminism itself." How then might the *homemaking films* from my grandmother's generation be understood in relation to the feminist avant-garde of the 1960s and 1970s? Likewise, if we concede that *homemaking films* were a part of the memory making and world building expected of women of my grandmother's generation, how might we see different possibilities in the world-building of contemporary transmedia authorship described by scholars such as Henry Jenkins?

From Genotype to Genealogy: Homemaking Noir, "Peter, Peter...," and *Trace Decay*

Many scholars insist on the significance of the generic conventions of home movies and photo albums over the idiosyncrasy of individual texts. In Patricia Eren's case study of the Galler home movies, for example, she cites Michael Lesy's work on family snapshots. He describes the effect of studying thousands of snapshots, saying, "You begin to lose track of people's individuality… you begin to think about genotypes."[11] This narrative of repetition runs the risk of effacing difference, reducing multiplicities into a singularity, and producing the "home movie" as an object as though it could be understood *a priori*. Yet, just as Roland Barthes suggests that society wants to tame the photograph by making it Art or generalizing away its confrontation and madness, I want to insist that the individuality and idiosyncrasy of each *homemaking* text holds

---

[11] Patricia Erens, "The Galler Home Movies: A Case Study," *Journal of Film and Video*, Summer/Fall (1986), 15. Filmmaker Alan Berliner repeats these observations in a recent episode of *This American Life*.

This Precarious Authorship: Some Notes on Home Movies,
Homemaking, and Alternative
the possibility not just of recognition, but of discovery.[12]

The first of my grandparents' movies were taken on their
honeymoon in 1941. They are camping, clearly taking turns
passing the camera back and forth. This honeymoon footage
provides a kind of baseline of their camera styles to compare
with subsequent footage when neither of them is in the frame.
In this, the earliest of their footage, all of the shots are of
roughly equal clarity in terms of focus and exposure, though
there are some differences in both their camerawork and their
performances. While not exactly guilty of what Maija Howe calls
a "photographic hangover," my grandfather's shots exhibit the
intentionality, pre-visualization, and control characteristic of his
still photography practice. His shots appear composed, they
tend to remain relatively still, and there is a clear use of
foreground and background. When onscreen, he always seems
to be playing to the camera: showing off, mugging, or refusing
direction. In contrast, my grandmother's shots are kinetic: they
move with her body and her eye. Her images feel more
relational than compositional, reproducing her glance and
reinscribing her point of view. When onscreen, she appears
relaxed and although at times she may be taking direction, she
does not self-consciously perform.

Once the honeymoon is over, so to speak, there is a clear
difference in clarity and duration between the images where my
grandfather holds the camera and those where my
grandmother does. My grandmother's images, which include
most of the footage of the children, are often fleeting, out of
focus, and underexposed. My grandfather and great uncle
Larry's relatively balanced, stable, and bright images suggest
the familial ideology so often associated with home movies of
the "daddy-filmer" era. My grandmother's show something else.
In one of the brightest and most magical of her fleeting
moments, my one or two-year-old mother balances in the palm

---

[12] Roland Barthes, *Camera Lucinda: Reflections on
Photography* (New York: Hill and Wang: 1981), 118.

of my grandfather's raised hand, precariously teetering as the camera abruptly cuts off. The abrupt cut-off is a hallmark of Grandmom's style: there are more important things than getting the shot. Perhaps the limitations of her footage are a visceral visualization of her activity of home*making* and mothering in the moment. Her footage is filled with dark shadowy babies with wide eyes and gaping mouths. While I can't say whether her chiaroscuro images were intentional, they certainly produce an iconography of the private *noir* of motherhood, filled with devouring darkness, bloody knees, and more children than hands. I do not know whether Grandmom was producing intentionally dark images. I do know that the last time I videotaped her, when she was in her late eighties and living in assisted living, she surprised me by asking if I had enough light and suggesting I try shooting from a different angle.

I used my grandmother's homemaking noir as the visual basis of my short film, "Peter, Peter…" The film is a retelling of the children's rhyme "Peter, Peter, Pumpkin Eater" using the vernacular conventions associated with home movies. Based loosely on the sensational Boston crime known as the Baked Ziti Murder, in which a husband kills and disembowels a wife over burnt pasta, the film might be described as a meditation on the question: How does a woman fit into a pumpkin shell? Researching the rhyme, I was fascinated by the quaint repetitions of domestic violence that the fairytale illustrations of a happy little woman in a pumpkin shell tried to undo. In children's rhymes, the relationship between text and image supersedes but never entirely erases the relationship between text and history, form, and content. In the rhyme, the violence is implicit and therefore acceptable: I was interested in making explicit the implicit violence that we are all raised within. Originally imagined as a pop-up book, the form was intended to relate the domestic space of the family (reading to children, home movies) to the pervasive cultural narratives that the children's rhyme invokes and reinscribes in endless iterations. By using the codes of the home movie, I situated the formal questions of the film in relation to larger questions of vernacular storytelling, domestic space, and the reiteration of—and resistance to—cultural narratives. These tropes, the unsteady camera, dark domestic interiors, and awkwardly edited sequences, were designed to inscribe questions of narration and point-of-view within the text of the film. Reproducing uncanny noir of my grandmother's homemaking movies was intended to undercut the nostalgia so often produced through home movies and emphasize the contrast between the voiceover narration and the narrative that unfolds. In retrospect, there are many predecessors to this work. At the time, however, I was making a personal film in relation to broad popular culture. I heard of Helen Franz's work shortly before I learned of Michelle Citron, Camille Billops, Jan Oxenberg, and Barbara Hammer, and long before I saw the work of Vivienne Dick, Cecelia Condit, and Zoe Beloff.

I returned to the family's home movies in *Trace Decay* (2009, multi-media, 60 minutes), a live collaborative experiment with my sister, choreographer Sasha Welsh; composer J Why; and performers Laurie Berg, Cindy Chung Camins, and Cynthia St. Clair. *Trace Decay* was developed through an intense improvisational process between the artist-performers and our/their home media including 8mm films, still photographs, VHS tapes, and audiocassettes. These movement-based performances explored processes of memory (both cultural and personal) and the experience of the passage of time.[13] We tried to work both with and against the media, allowing enjoyment of its sentimental seduction or absurdity while also disrupting and transforming it. In the end of the first section, for example, as we moved from the austere black and white of the earliest films

---

[13] The development of Trace Decay was supported by The Swarthmore Project, a residency program for choreographers and dancers sponsored by Swarthmore College in Swarthmore, PA. Trace Decay was presented at Triskelion Arts, Brooklyn, NY, and Window on the Work at Swarthmore College. Excerpts have been shown at RAW Material at Dance New Amsterdam, Body Blend at Dixon Place, Open Performance at Dance Theatre Workshop, and Movement Media's Kinetic Cinema.

into the lush bleeding colors of 1940s swimmers and picnickers, the nostalgic images accelerate until they are cut as single-frames. Using footage that was shot with a video camera from live projection with projector sound, this acceleration of cuts created a violence in the soundtrack that transformed the recognizable whir of the home movie projector into the abrupt and machine-like sounds of war. These home movies were made in wartime. My grandfather did shift work at Martins, where they manufactured the planes that would drop atomic bombs on Hiroshima and Nagasaki. I remember live wrangling the projector to stream the almost lyrical image of my great-aunt Bernie in front of an impossibly blue ocean directly onto Cindy Chung Camins' body. She completely rejected the nostalgic lure of the image, declaring that her family's memories don't look like that.

On Homemaking Histories, the Refusal of Repetition, and Taking the Camera

My grandmother's philosophy of cultural texts in relation to returning and repetition was direct and unequivocal: "I don't even look at the old movies on the television, you know. If I've seen it I don't want to see it again." She emphasized and repeated this refusal: first, she used the example of *It's a Wonderful Life*, which she referred to as "that Christmas one," saying, "I saw it once and that was it." Then to expand and drive home her point, she declared, "I don't read a book over again either. Once I've read it, I wouldn't read it over."

Within the context of my grandmother's home economics, these refusals of repetition are best understood in relation to the value of time and of new experiences. If culture accumulates power through reinscription, repetition, and return, the refusal of repetition makes space for the new. Yet, by returning to my grandmother's memory, reviewing and reinscribing her once forgotten homemaking films, and repeating her surreptitiously recorded words, new perspectives, pleasures, and possibilities are produced. These are not simply nostalgic documents of the sentimental ideology of the nuclear family, but fragments of

This Precarious Authorship: Some Notes on Home Movies, Homemaking, and Alternative

other, idiosyncratic histories and ways of seeing. They do not document what Don Slater has called, "the right family," but rather inscribe the everyday glance of a busy mother of five, before the camera abruptly shuts off. Not unlike the moon my Grandpop made me under the stairs as a child, my grandmother's homemaking films remind us that we cannot see the truth: there's only magic, only making.

Long after the years my grandmother was tasked with the unwanted job of taking moving pictures of her growing family, my uncle David—who would later give me the gift of my grandmother's films—bought a home video camera. In one of his tapes from the 1980s, he records a gathering of the extended family at the swim club. There's Grandmom, looking into the camera. Uncle David tries to convince her to get into the pool so that he can tape her swimming. She flatly refuses, and then reverses his direction, saying, "*You* get in the pool."

"I can't," he counters. "I have the camera."

Grandmom doesn't miss a beat as she replies, "Oh, I'll take the camera."

Laura Mulvey
For Terry Braunstein (2015)
Kate Lain

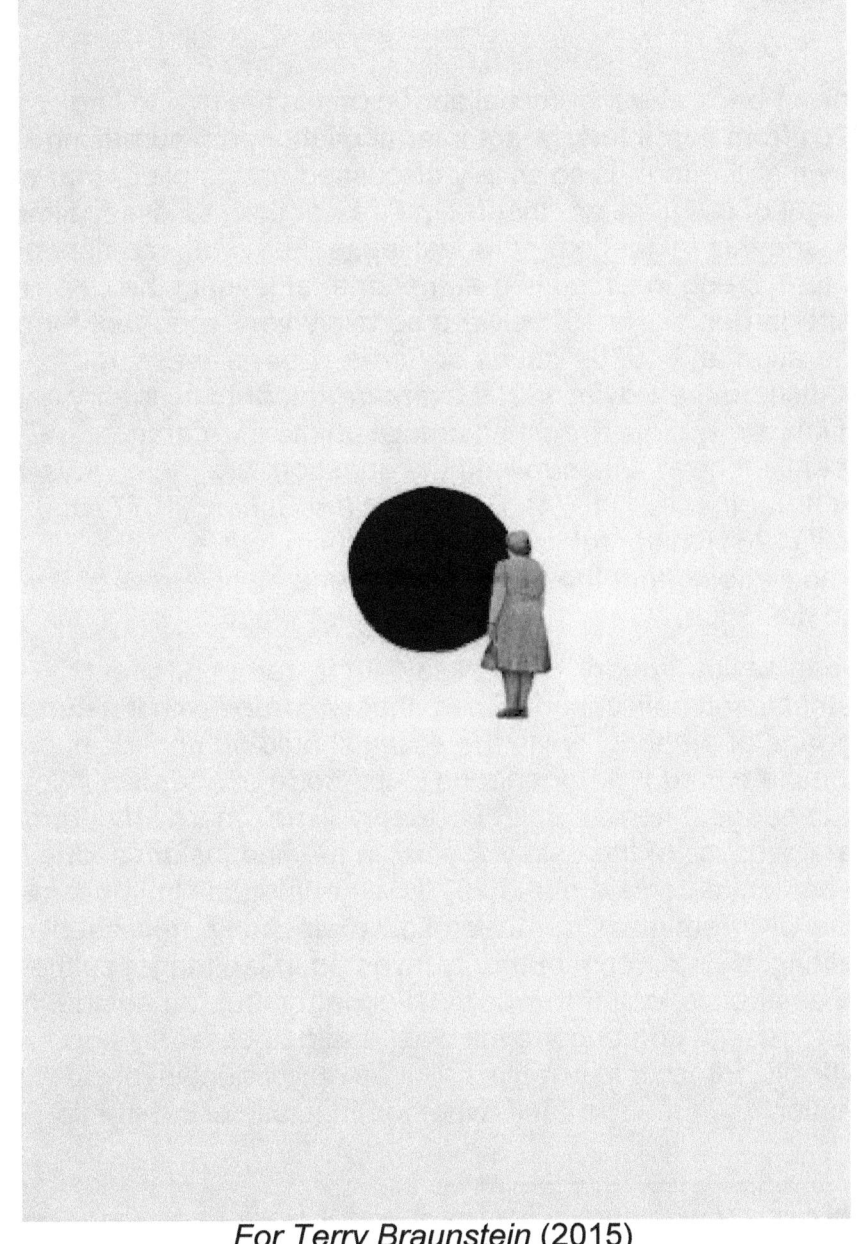

For Terry Braunstein (2015)
paper, hole, possibility

Peter Wollen, Laura Mulvey: "theory" film as essay film?

Laura Mulvey

Looking back at our early collaborations in the mid to late 1970s from some forty years later, it might seem surprising (now that the term is so widely discussed and applied) that we thought of our films as "theoretical" rather than as essay films. But, and this might be a personal lapse, I have no memory of the term being in circulation at the time, at least in the UK. The avant-gardes of the 1920s were certainly very important for our generation and 1970s issues of *Screen* bear witness, for instance, to the Soviet 1920s avant-garde, both its theory and its films, as well as Brecht as crucial points of reference. Recently, I have asked myself the question: are there ways in which *Penthesilea* (1974), *Riddles of the Sphinx* (1977) and *AMY!* (1981) might relate to the essay film (while acknowledging that the very flexibility and elusiveness of the form defines it)?[1]

To begin with, "theory" and "essay" imply rather different aesthetic and political principles: theory carries with it a certain baggage of authority while the essay should be uncertain, incomplete, and heterogeneous in its mode of address. I would like to suggest here that, if our "theory films" shared the formal characteristics of the essay, it was, in the first instance, due to the particular context of the 1970s experimental film movement in the UK. Feminism, our theoretical mainspring, necessarily challenged patriarchal authority invested in language, culture, and aesthetics; out of this political engagement, an aesthetic of heterogeneity and uncertainty was, again necessarily and politically, intrinsic to our films. But as our project involved questioning language itself, whether linguistic or cinematic, how

---

[1] This essay was originally published for Nora Alter and Timothy Corrigan, eds., *Essays on the Essay Film* (forthcoming, Columbia University Press).

ideas became words or images, a theoretical dimension was also fundamental to the films.

2. Some personal background.

Peter and I were both writing about film from a theoretical perspective before we ever imagined that we would make films ourselves. Our writing was, however, "essayistic": quite short pieces published in journals and magazines, outside either a film criticism or an academic context, with personal commitment and original ideas compensating for the lack of footnotes or in depth research. Peter's early film writing in the 1960s had reflected his *Cahiers du Cinema* influenced Hollywood period (which had, in turn, influenced me). His 1969 *Signs and Meaning in the Cinema* (definitely a work of serious research although still light on footnotes) is an obvious turning point: the book is a triptych of three essays, with "auteurism" sandwiched between Eisenstein and film semiotics. It acts as a signpost, indicating that his interests were moving away from the great Hollywood directors towards the avant-garde and film theory.

Then, around the same time and just as Peter became more and more preoccupied with Godard's radical films of the late 60s/early 70s, New American Cinema, new radical European cinemas, Brazil's Cinema Novo etc. also reached the UK through festivals, special seasons and so on. All these cinemas, and perhaps Godard above all, showed that films could be made about ideas and depict thought and that the paraphernalia of large productions were neither necessary or relevant. My turning point came later with the influence of the Women's Movement; writing "Visual Pleasure and Narrative Cinema" in 1973/4 marked my break with Hollywood and my new interest in experimental cinema, which was, in the first instance, the small but heroic tradition of women's experimental cinema. But these personal, intellectual and political shifts would not, as such, have enabled us to make films ourselves. It was the wider intellectual context in the UK in the 70s, backed institutionally by new funding sources, that brought a new

Peter Wollen, Laura Mulvey: "theory" film as essay film? movement of radical experimental film into existence. For Peter and me, it was a logical step to apply for available funding, to expand our written theoretical essays into image and sound; we could then reflect cinematically on the kinds of political and cultural film issues and questions that we wanted to explore. Laura Rascaroli quotes Hans Richter's concept of the essay film as providing "images for mental notions" and "portray a concept":

> In the effort to give body to the invisible world of imagination, thought and ideas, the essay film can employ an incomparably greater reservoir of expressive means than can the pure documentary film. Freed from recording external phenomena in simple sequence the film essay must collect it material from everywhere; its space and time conditioned only by the need to explain and show the idea.[2]

Although we were unaware of these useful essay film aesthetic guidelines and principles, they coincide quite closely with our aspirations at the time.

3. Principles: some points of coincidence between theory film and essay film.

As Peter and I worked in collaboration, we designed our films as much as possible in advance and, by and large, in accordance with certain agreed principles. The idea of "theory" as the main driving force of these "compositions" was, as I said above, an extension of our earlier essays but was also completely different due to the move into the film medium. I remember Peter used the concept in the Marxist sense: political activity could range across theory, agit-prop and propaganda. But he had also a longstanding interest in avant-garde art,

---

[2] Laura Rascaroli, *The Personal Camera: Subjective Cinema and the Essay Film* (London: Wallflower, 2009), 24-5.

---

literature and modernism, predating and alongside his interest in film. He made a characteristic point in an interview in *Screen,* soon after we made *Penthesilea*:

> One of the objects of the film, to my mind anyway, is to say that people should be prepared to make the same effort and approach a film in the same way as they would a book. It is a text, and just as when people read a book they are prepared to do further reading or they are prepared to encounter difficulties, so they should in a film. That is implicit in the transfer of the idea of reading... One could call our film a political film in the sense that one, for instance, would talk about Brecht as producing political texts. You can also argue that people like Lautreamont or Joyce or Duchamp were political in another sense, subversive or deconstructive, although they professed no interest in politics at all. And our film shows as much influence from, eg, Duchamp as it does from Brecht - perhaps more.

Our working principles indicate hybrid influences as well as a commitment to an aesthetic of hybridity. The films should be heterogeneous, broken into chapters, made up of very different kinds of material that had to include found footage, direct address to camera and a foregrounding of medium specificity. The films had to be hybrid in their citation of other arts, quoting, for instance, visual arts and including music, but also, probably most importantly, incorporating words and language, as image and voice. They also had to include some element of storytelling and performance.

3. Language, writing and psychoanalytic theory

Although these strategies might have a lot in common with those of some essay films, they were applied to very definitely theoretical topics. From rather different perspectives, Peter and I were both concerned with questions that had been thrown up

Peter Wollen, Laura Mulvey: "theory" film as essay film? by feminism. In our first two films, we used two ancient Greek myths of monstrous women (Amazons and the Sphinx) as hooks on which to hang reflections on women's place within patriarchal culture, language and the "Symbolic Order" (to use the Lacanian term). Through a Women's Liberation reading group, I had encountered Freud and psychoanalysis and it seemed as though Freudian theory could offer a way in, like a small crack of light through a chink in a door, and illuminate some of the problems that early feminist theory was trying to address; psychoanalytic concepts and their vocabulary were extremely relevant to questions of gender, sexuality and now they were socialized under patriarchy. Peter and I wanted to use the myth of the Sphinx to question the Freudian Oedipus Complex, displacing the Oedipal father with the problem of motherhood. This idea runs through *Riddles* like a central spine but still allowed digression into varying modes of address and reflections on the mother/child relation in everyday as well as theoretical terms.

In both *Penthesilea* and *Riddles of the Sphinx*, Peter and I were particularly preoccupied with language, both as an aesthetic tool and as a topic of investigation in its own right. Lacan's reformulation of the Freudian Oedipus Complex into the successive phases of Imaginary (maternal and pre-language) and Symbolic (paternal and post-language) seemed, to a feminist mentality, to sum up perfectly the dilemma of motherhood and its place not only in the oppressions of the everyday but also crucially formative for patriarchal culture. We were influenced by the French feminist theorists, Julia Kristeva and Luce Irigaray, both of whom questioned the Lacanian Oedipal chronology and the rigid distinction between the pre and post Oedipal. Kristeva's concept of the "semiotic" associates the maternal body with a pre-Symbolic form signification: these tones and rhythms of language, later become subordinated to the purpose of denotative meaning but also persist in poetic writing and music. Our interest in language and the verbal was a logical development of this theoretical and mythic background. In the first instance, "language" meant the lack of it, suggesting an in-between space in which to reflect on how muteness might be made apparent or find a mode of expression. Although the relation between speech and non-speech is crucial to *Penthesilea*, in *Riddles of the Sphinx* words take on new importance so that the verbal and the visual intertwine, "reaching out towards" or "on the verge of" expressiveness, and asking: how does the verbal function within the "muteness" of the semiotic?

Although apropos Godard"s *Le Gai Savoir,* in "The Two Avant-gardes" Peter elaborates the point, which was to become essential for the questions addressed in our films:

> ... the film [*Le Gai Savoir*] deliberately suspends 'meaning', avoids any teleology or finality, in the interests of a destruction and reassembly, a re-combination of the order of the sign as an experiment in the dissolution of old meanings and the generation of new ones from the semiotic process itself... *Le Gai Savoir* is not a film with a meaning, something to say about the world, nor is it a film "about" film... but a film about the possibility of meaning itself, of generating new types of meaning. The array of sign-systems at work in the cinema are thus brought into a new kind of relationship with each other and with the world.

Located within the context of *Riddles* and its commitment to considering the "problem" of motherhood, "the possibility of meaning itself, of generating new types of meaning... a new kind of relationship with each other and the world" all lead to a search for the place from which women could utter the repressed counter-meanings of patriarchal discourse, an area of experiment in its own right, a theoretical move away from linguistic transparency to the stutter, the hieroglyph and the riddle.

Quotation from our notes on *Riddles:*

> The 'voice' of the Sphinx has special significance, speaking from a distinct place with a distinct form

Peter Wollen, Laura Mulvey: "theory" film as essay film?

> of language. The riddle is metaphoric, interrogative, and incomplete; it involves wordplay, enigma, and disguise. It is, however, important to stress that the Sphinx is not outside language as she is outside the city of Thebes, the realm of patriarchy, but is able to offer a different discourse, potentially the nucleus of a non-patriarchal symbolic, based on a different Oedipal structure-or, perhaps it would be better to say, a different mode of entry into language, kinship, and history. Language is the component of film that both threatens to regulate the spectator and also offers the hope of liberation from the closed world of identification and the lure of the image. Language, therefore, is both a friend and a foe, against which we must be on our guard, whose help we need but whose claims we must combat. Hence the body of language in our films is fractured and dislodged.

To my mind, these kinds of ideas and the questions associated with them share the sense of uncertainty, experiment and the essay as "attempt" that many commentators have seen as central to the essay film aesthetic. Furthermore, the different kinds of "voice" embodied in the Sphinx shift from the questions of theory to questions of form and its disembodied voice, the voiceover, is characteristic of many essay films. But the Sphinx's voice moves through a variety of discourses: the fragmented association of words with the domestic space at the beginning of the narrative section of the film, to a series of theoretical and practical problems raised by motherhood in everyday life, and finally, in the last two pans of "Louise's Story," to a dream-like, experimental form of writing. Peter was, throughout, the primary writer for both *Penthesilea* and *Riddles* as he was, as I was not, a writer of poetry and stories as well as essays and specifically interested in experimental writing. For the "mirror" sequence (the twelfth pan) he used a method loosely adapted from the surrealist writer Raymond Roussel. He cross-referenced words between French and English dictionaries, then taking the word that came on the line below, and collected an arbitrary vocabulary and a random sequence of phrases that were then re-written into an apparent narrative. It was not so much that Peter intended to emulate dream language or the language of the unconscious, but rather to generate words, and images from words, that foregrounded a linguistic materiality in the same sense that avant-garde film had always foregrounded the materiality of its medium.

4. Self-expression and audience.

Peter and I were not, as collaborators, particularly concerned with self-expression; our long and detailed discussions merged quite diverse backgrounds and priorities into a framework for mutual aesthetic and political agreement. The author and his or her self and its expression was under erasure at this time from multiple directions, for instance, early post-modernism, feminism, and Roland Barthes. In this sense, our films diverge from the sense of self-expression so often associated with the essay film. However, although there was no "self" to make itself felt, direct address (PW in *Penthesilea,* LM in *Riddles*, both in *AMY!)* was one of our cinematic strategies or principles, more to mark the process of the text's construction, that is more Brechtian, than coming from a specific individual. But more to the point, perhaps, was a conscious address to an audience, which we visualized, at its core, as belonging to the same milieu as we did, that is: aware of the significance of feminism for that political moment, a shared belief in the importance of the questions that feminism raised, both for the cinema and for everyday life, committed to the political radicalism of avant-garde aesthetics, their challenge to the transparency of dominant ways of seeing and the offer of a poetic, visual, cinematic novelty and excitement to anyone who cared to give the films a try. We always conceived, perhaps optimistically, of the core as porous, essentially a gateway to the so-called and always elusive "wider audience" but realistically these films neither could or would reach beyond a limited constituency. While our first two films' running time of 90 minutes made a

Peter Wollen, Laura Mulvey: "theory" film as essay film? residual gesture to the feature film, our concern for mise-en-scene was much more significantly rooted in Hollywood: color, lighting, camera movement, music, gesture and contrasts between interior and exterior spaces and perspectives, for instance, were designed to be "read" by the spectator, in the manner of the 1950s melodrama that I had loved so much. *Riddles* has a carefully constructed symmetrical pattern, evoking a pyramid, with rhyming sequences arranged on each side of a central pivot point. In addition to the "Contents Page" at the beginning of the film, we hoped that this pattern would offer the spectator a structure within which he or she could find an orientation in the face of the difficulty and the heterogeneity presented by the material. If the emphasis on mise-en-scene had Douglas Sirk or Vicente Minnelli in mind, the pattern of the film was influenced by Hollis Frampton's use of structure in *Zorms Lemma* or *("nostalgia")*. Finally, the sections of Louise's Story that move onto location, introduce chance elements: casual passers-by, the wind blowing in the trees, circulating traffic, which related more to Italian Neo-realism and, for Peter and me, most particularly to Roberto Rossellini. Although we had no expectation that these cinematic citations would be picked up by an actual audience... we could always imagine that they just might have been.

FILMS MENTIONED IN THIS ESSAY:

Penthesilea: Queen of the Amazons (UK, 1974, 99mins, 16mm, Color)
Director: Laura Mulvey and Peter Wollen
Screenplay: Laura Mulvey and Peter Wollen
Cinematography: Louis Castelli
Editor: Larry Sider
Sound: Larry Sider
Cast: Peter Wollen Grace, McKeaney, Debra Dolansky, Michael Thomas, Jan
Creighton, Jim Goode, Lisa Kephart, Pat Kerwin, Whit MacLaughlin, Kristine

Laura Mulvey
Nielsen, Brian Reich, Jerry Stropnicky, Ann Woodworth, voice
of Jessie Ashley
Video sequence: Evanston Percussion Unit
Produced by: Laura Mulvey and Peter Wollen
Source of Print: British Film Institute
Language: English

Penthesilea: Queen of the Amazons (Mulvey's first film, co-
directed with Peter Wollen) explores her fascination with Greek
culture through the myth of the Amazonian Queen. Inspired by
Heinrich von Kleist's 1808 play about the Amazonian queen, in
Mulvey and Wollen's piece the myth of Penthesilea reinforces
the 1970s political struggle through an investigation of the
position of the "heroic" woman within cultural history.
Penthesilea forms the first part of a trilogy, followed by *Riddles
of the Sphinx* and *AMY!,* both of which are shown in this year's
Experiments in Cinema Festival.

Riddles of the Sphinx (UK, 1977, 92mins, 16mm, Color)
Director: Laura Mulvey and Peter Wollen
Screenplay: Laura Mulvey and Peter Wollen
Cinematography: Diane Tammes
Sound: Larry Sider
Editing: Larry Sider, assisted by Carola Klein
Music: Mike Ratledge
Cast: Dinah Stabb, Laura Mulvey, Merdelle Jordine, Riannon
Tise, Clive Merrison,
Marie Green, Paula Melbourne, Crissie Trigger, Mary Maddox,
Mary Kelly
Producer: Keith Griffiths
Produced by: British Film Institute
Source of Print: British Film Institute
Language: English

In this most celebrated of Mulvey and Wollen's films, the story
of a young mother Louise is told in 360° pans that depict the
protagonist's everyday life: her marriage, her encounters with
friends and family. Filmed in seven sections, the Sphinx
functions as an abstract narrator, and the film constitutes the

Peter Wollen, Laura Mulvey: "theory" film as essay film? embodiment of Mulvey and Wollen's critical investigations of film.

AMY! (UK, 1980, 30mins, 16mm, color; black and white)
Director: Laura Mulvey and Peter Wollen
Screenplay: Laura Mulvey and Peter Wollen
Cinematography: Diane Tammes
Editor: Larry Sider
Sound: Larry Sider
Cast: Mary Maddox, the voice of Yvonne Rainer
Producer: Patsy Nightingale
Produced by: Modelmark for South East Arts Association
Source of print: ACE
Language: English

"Happy the land that needs no heroes," Bertold Brecht once said. AMY!, the last part of Mulvey and Wollen's loose trilogy, after Penthesilea and Riddles of the Sphinx, contemplates ways in which societies create heroines. The pioneering English aviatrix Amy Johnson gained fame in 1930 after her legendary solo flight from Britain to Australia and the film marks its 50th anniversary. Johnson's persona is explored through the use of various fictional images, sounds and readings of her private letters. Set in the 1980s, the music by legendary punk formation Poly Styrene and X-Ray Spex, marks the conceptual rather than historical nature of the film.

Curation, synopsis, and biographical notes by Kamila Kuc.

BIOGRAPHICAL NOTES:

Laura Mulvey
Born in Oxford in 1941, Mulvey studied History at Oxford University. In 1975 she published "Visual Pleasure and Narrative Cinema," a highly influential psychoanalytic feminist polemic on the voyeuristic systems of spectatorship found in Hollywood film. Mulvey made six films with Peter Wollen that attempted to counteract these patriarchal structures including *Riddles of the Sphinx* (1977), *Frida Kahlo and Tina Modotti*

Laura Mulvey

(1982), and *The Bad Sister* (1983). She has written extensively on Sirk, Godard, and Hitchcock and remains a pre-eminent authority on film theory. Her recent book *Death 24x a Second* looks at the impact of new media technologies on shifting modes of film spectatorship. She is currently Professor of Film and Media Studies at Birkbeck College, University of London.

Peter Wollen
Born in London in 1938, Wollen studied English at Oxford. His influential book *Signs and Meanings in Cinema* (1965) constitutes a reflection of his interests in the politics of the New Left, semiotic film theory, Russian avant-garde, the French New Wave, and Freudian and Lacanian psychoanalysis. Wollen remains one of the leading theorists on avant-garde film and he also co-wrote Michelangelo Antonioni's *The Passenger* (1975). Between 1974 and 1983, he made six films with Laura Mulvey. His own feature, *Friendship's Death* (1987), is a futuristic story set in Amman in September 1970 during the battles between Palestinian guerrillas and the Jordanian army.

Kamila Kuc
An academic, curator, and experimental filmmaker. Forthcoming is her monograph *The Promises of the Avant-Garde: Polish Experiments in Film from Expressionism to Constructivism* (Indiana University Press, 2016). Kuc has previously curated Laura Mulvey for the New Horizons Film Festival in Wroclaw, Poland (2010, accompanied by the first in Polish collection of Mulvey's essays, co-edited by Kuc). She is currently a Post-doctoral Research Fellow at Goldsmiths, University of London. Her films have been screened at the Alternative Film/Video in Belgrade, Serbia; Experiments in Cinema Festival, Albuquerque, New Mexico; and Haverhill Experimental Film Festival. Last year her film *Rehearsal* (2014) was nominated for the VGIK Award at the Blow-Up Arthouse Film Fest, Chicago, Illinois. She is the recipient of such prestigious grants as the Arts and Humanities Research

Peter Wollen, Laura Mulvey: "theory" film as essay film?
Council, and most recently, Arts Council England/British
Council Artists' International Development Fund.

Kamila Kuc
Ciné, ma vérité: Memory as a Creative Force in the Process of Constructing Subjectivities
Kamila Kuc

Woman must write her self: must write about women and bring women to writing, from which they have been driven away as violently as from their bodies—for the same reasons, by the same law, with the same fatal goal. Woman must put herself into the text—as into the world and into history—by her own movement.
Hélène Cixous, "The Laugh of the Medusa" (1975)

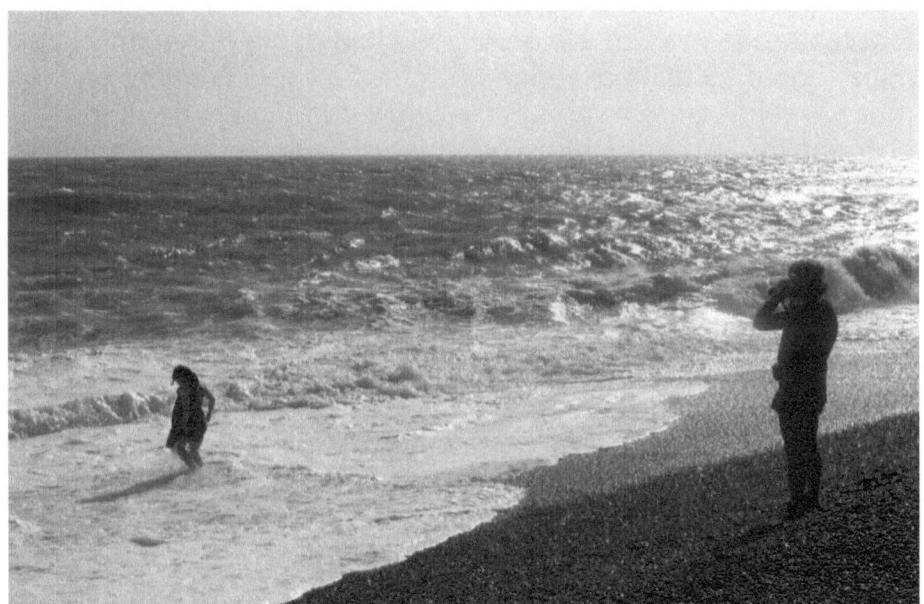

Batum (2015), production still. © Daisy Rickman. Putting ourselves into the text: *Batum*'s entirely female crew: Genie Kaminski (actress/voice artist), Nina Zabicka (second camera), Daisy Rickman (stills photographer), and myself.

******

I owe the first part of this essay's title to Chris Marker's witty word pun on the tradition of cinéma vérité. I chose Marker's phrase because it challenges the notion of any collective cine-

Ciné, ma vérité: Memory as a Creative Force in the Process of Constructing Subjectivities

truth, as proposed by Dziga Vertov in his theory of Kino-Pravda, for example. Instead, Marker alludes to the inability of film to capture any truths beyond a filmmaker's own subjective experiences of the world.

******

The main impulse behind this essay is to explore some of the themes and methods I employed in *Batum* (2015, Super8, 12 mins), a film that takes as its starting point my personal experience of near drowning in the Black Sea of Batumi, Georgia. As such, *Batum* is induced with a desire for an auto-ethnographical self-interrogation as I wish to move towards creating a personal cartography of my experiences. Images that feature in the film are a constellation of memories that are mine (one may think of Roland Barthes' *punctum* here), and those that I acquired through the knowledge of history and culture (Barthes' *studium*). The latter ones I call *prosthetic*, and they are exemplified here by the poems of Osip Mandelstam and Joseph Stalin, among other cultural tropes. Mikhail Bulgakov's unpublished play *Batum* reasonates throughout my film, least of all in its title. While making *Batum* I was set to explore a certain displacement of identity that emerges when we encounter past experiences. I sought to *experience* how memories become fiction once recorded and how in this process of recording, the camera itself held a mysterious agency. I am, above all, always interested in ways in which film, as one of the technologies of memory, can be seen as an innovative creator of memories themselves. The complex relationship between personal and collective memories often subverts the social and political identity constructions, which I tend to explore in my films.

Kamila Kuc
******

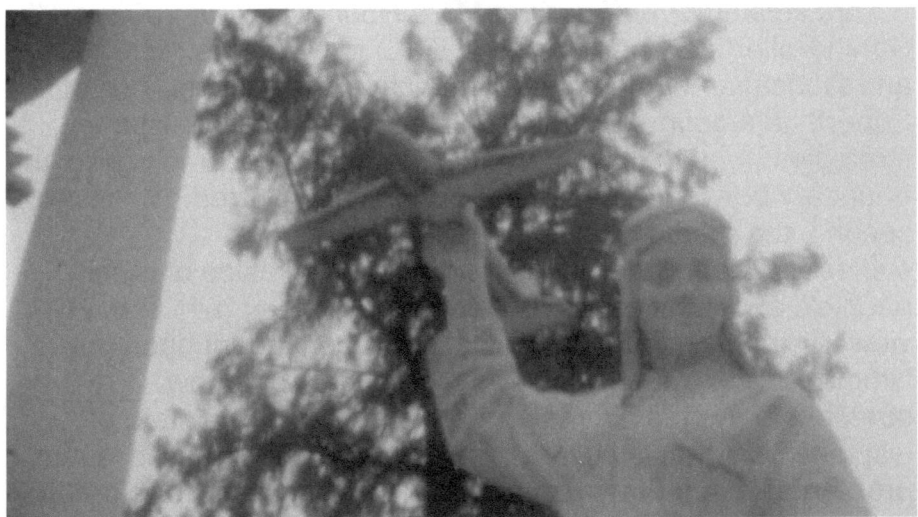

Rob Godman's authorial "thinking underwater" sound is merged with a remix of Georgia's 1918-1920 National Anthem.

A large part of *Batum* relies on affect that was created through a careful sound composition mastered by Rob Godman. We wanted to imagine how it is to be able to hear and "think" underwater. Remembering is always accompanied by forgetting as memory remembers and neglects and nobody really knows how it is to hear underwater. At this point the film's original, inherent silence was met with an artificially created sound. This process reflected upon a general sense of displacement in *Batum*—displacement of images and sound, as well as of identity. This way both sound and image are united by fiction. They gradually become more fictional as memories of the past merge with various trajectories of the present.

******

Memories are fragile beings. They are most of all unreliable and depend upon our current cirumstance; they carry an aura of an irrecoverable loss and dereliction—just like Super8 film does. Invented to *create* (home) memories, Super8 was supposed to preserve them, i.e. preserve positive images of family life for posterity. I think here of Alina Marazzi's delicate

Ciné, ma vérité: Memory as a Creative Force in the Process of Constructing Subjectivities

Un'ora sola ti vorrei (*For One More Hour with You*, 2002) and Sarah Polley's *Stories We Tell* (2012) in which the *recreation* and *fabrication* of memories, respectively, signify the use of Super8 as a defining measure of the filmmakers' artistic strategies. In both films, personal memories become public; the boundary between private and collective is blurred. For a split second, the medium undergoes a process of de-subjectivization. Time is suspended and fantasies of other people's experiences can be recreated as their own in many viewers' minds. "Truth," in any case, is contingent upon the filmmaker and the audience as memory is somehow stretchable. As the filmmaker herself remains in a state of displacement that is cultural, geographic, and linguistic, such process of momentary disorientation is necessary for a creation of any subjectivity within a film that takes memory as its core theme. Self-reflexivity, too, constitutes a deliberate artistic strategy that contributes to the demystification of the filmmaking process itself and illuminates the filmmaker's ideological position.

******

The past is realized in and through the present as memories have a tendency to invade our consciousness. Still alive, they often cause a disruption in and to the present. I was unaware of the complexities of this process until the editing of *Batum* began. In order to access certain parts of one's memories, a filmmaker must become—in Walter Benjamin's words—an archaeologist, "a man digging" and a person who returns "again and again to the same matter." The previously hidden and highly sought after images may then emerge "like precious fragments or torsos in a collector's gallery" preserved for our "later understanding." Benjamin's vanishing point of history doesn't reside in a distant past, but rather in the present. The conventional view of history as receding somewhere behind us and disappearing into a nonexistent time is challenged here by Benjamin's claim that the vanishing point of history can always be found in the present moment. I am also reminded here of Vladimir Nabokov's seduction of the past whose demands

Kamila Kuc

cannot be balanced by the future, since the future does not exist. In *Batum*, existence is suspended between past, present, and unattainable future; there is only contingency and no certainty; perspectives shift continuously as we attempt to escape fixation. In *Batum*, subjectivity is negotiated through memory: cinematic time identifies itself with psychological time as editing aligns itself with memory.

******

Memory and imagination are intertwined. Imagination translates sensory data into mental images but it is also capable of producing images independently. Imagination, to some degree, facilitates memory's desire to come to the surface. While investigating one's relationship to one's personal history, a certain syncopation, physical and otherwise, can be witnessed in the process of recreating versions of events. Here documentary-like elements blend with fiction. For Jean-Luc Godard "all great fictional films tend towards documentary, just as all great documentaries tend towards fiction." A mélange of the two invites a possibility of exploiting multiple forms of subjectivity since there are as many truths and realities as there are filmmakers (and viewers). To this end, we can only speak of identifications, not identities.

******

Filmmaking is a process of mediation; thus, the access to any form of authentic past is denied by default. *Batum* grants a superficial entry to a past experience, but can never render it present. The experience will always remain elusive.

******

Ciné, ma vérité: Memory as a Creative Force in the Process of Constructing Subjectivities

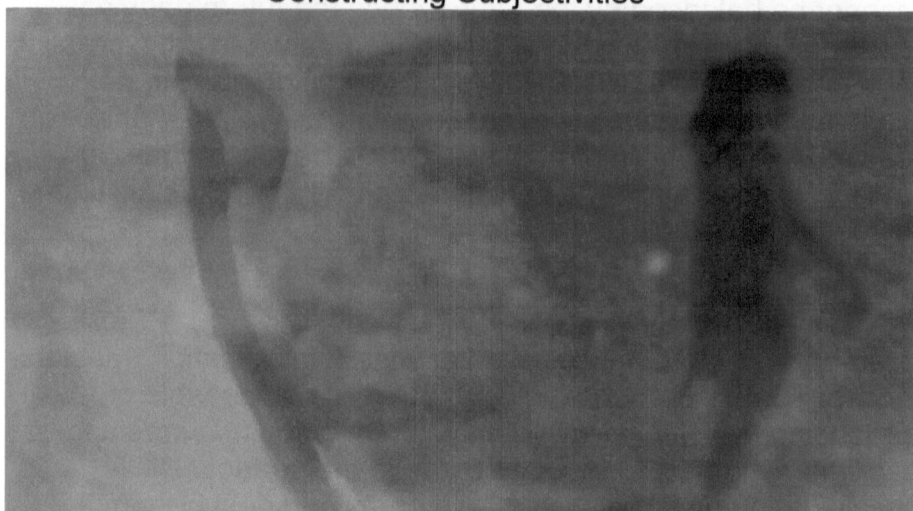

Reenacting the past: restaging of subjectivities, Genie Kaminski.

Genie Kaminski reenacted the parts of my near drowning, and provided a luminous Russian voice for Mandelstam and Stalin's poems. Restaging of the events and memories constitutes a restaging of my own subjectivity. Needless to say, this reenactment is not a duplication of the original event. It can never be. It is a snapshot of, a metaphorical close-up on, a detail that is crucial to the film's skeleton. When used in a non-narrative, non-fiction context, performance further underlines the impossibility of any authentic representation. Performativity itself is a strategy. The subject who is filming is the one whose life is being reenacted, i.e. created in front of her eyes. The presence of a director manifests itself in her physical absence, but it is *embodied* in the movements of the camera. The camera is a tool in self-inscription as the filmmaker's own authorial voice is channeled through the scripted titles and chosen images.

******

Perhaps it is not life itself that creates autobiography. Instead, the actual process of writing and making invites life to unfold itself for us to record, i.e. to create. Filming life in retrospect (in a narrative or non-narrative form) is a creation rather than representation of that life. The impulse to tell a story gives life a shape; it produces its multiple versions. The apparatus itself has an agency: in *Peeping Tom* Mark Lewis' most defining moments are intensified only when he is looking through the lens. It is the apparatus itself that creates (records) and destroys life (the tripod's knife kills the women as Lewis is seen filming them in a close-up) at the same time. A film's camera is thus not an objective piece of machinery; *she* is an active agent in the process of formulating a story.

******

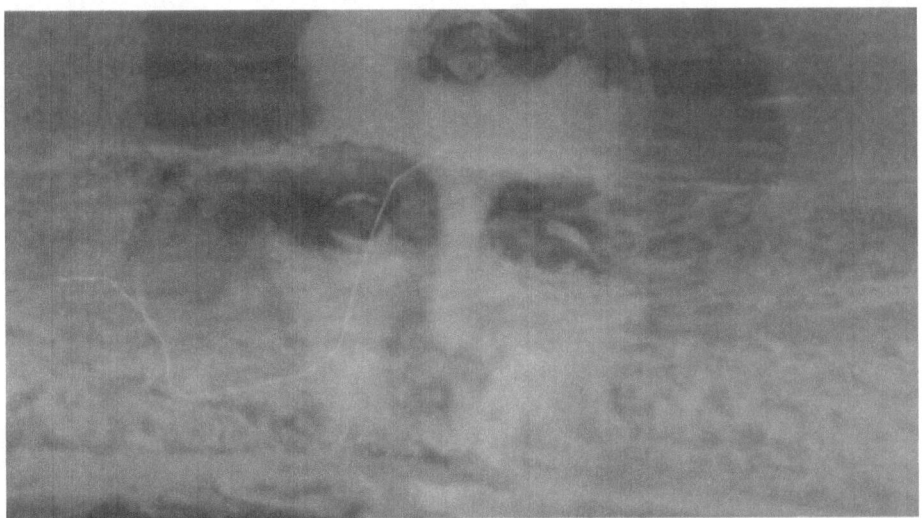

Stalin's "To the Moon" and Mandelstam's "Epigram Against Stalin" are recited by Genie Kaminski.

Batum is an attempt at offering a glimpse into my experience of near drowning. While making the film, I became aware of how entangled I was not only with the forces of nature, but more violently, with the forces of History. As Judith Butler states: "When the 'I' seeks to give an account of itself, it can start with itself, but it will find that this self is already implicated in a social temporality that exceeds its own capacities for narration: indeed, when the 'I' seeks to give an account of itself, an

Ciné, ma vérité: Memory as a Creative Force in the Process of Constructing Subjectivities

account that must include the conditions of its own emergence, it must as a matter of necessity, become a social theorist."

****

Biographical note:

Kamila Kuc (www.kamilakuc.com), Ph.D., is a writer, experimental filmmaker, and curator. She is currently a Postdoctoral Research Fellow in the Department of Media and Communications at Goldsmiths, University of London. She publishes widely on the subject of film and media. Her films have been screened at international film festivals, including Experiments in Cinema. She is the 2016 Basement Films Artist in Residence.

Bibliography:

Barad, Karen, *Meeting the Universe Halfway: Quantum Physics and the Entanglement of Matter and Meaning* (Durham: Duke University Press, 2007).

Barthes, Roland, *Camera Lucida: Reflections on Photography* (London: Vintage Classics, 1993) [1981].

Benjamin, Walter, "Berlin Chronicle," *One-way Street, and Other Writings* (London: New Left Books, 1979) [1932].

Birnbaum, Daniel, *Chronology* (New York/Berlin: Lukas & Sternberg, 2005).

Butler, Judith, *Giving an Account of Oneself* (New York: University Press, 2005).

Chivoiu, Oana, "Toward an Aesthetic of Displacement in Ana Vaz's *Sacris Pulso*," *Senses of Cinema*, Issue 68, Sept. 2013.

Cixous, Hélène, "The Laugh of the Medusa," *Signs*, Vol. 1, No.

therefore, we question the merits of "interdisciplinarity" rhetoric that has become a mainstay of research and teaching activity in the academy and beyond.

What follows is a series of documents and musings that should be read as interlacing conversations: neither an advisory admonition, nor evidence of a *rapprochement*, rather, our attempt to retrace our misadventures in working together at the edges of theory (Eva) and practice (Nina). Moreover, we do not mean these accounts to encapsulate "a theory" of either avant-garde film or transgender representation, but to describe a series of creative experiences that have brought a feminist experimental filmmaker, a transwoman writer/scholar, and the so-called "filmic apparatus" into proliferating, bumptious conversations for an extended period of time.

Genealogy of a Troubled Film

[Nina]: In 1995, several years before I met Eva Hayward, I began work on a film tentatively titled "Radiant Eyes." An experimental filmmaker with twenty years' experience, my previous work, including *Empathy* (1980), *Some Phases of An Empire* (1984), *Department of the Interior* (1987), *A Knowledge They Cannot Lose* (1989), and *The Accursed Mazurka* (1994), had explored dimensions of feminism and autobiography through densely layered and poetic uses of images and sounds. "Radiant Eyes" was initially inspired by my readings of essays about the advent of photography and some fictions from nineteenth-century French decadent and symbolist movements, such as Théophile Gautier's 1835 novel *Mademoiselle de Maupin,* Villiers de l'Isle-Adam's *L'eve Future* (*Eve of the Future Eden*, 1894), and Joris-Karl Huysmans À *Rebours* (*Against Nature*, 1884). From these readings, I conceived the film, in part, as a way to puzzle out the role photographic representation has played in perpetuating romanticized ideals of loving that are predicated on distance and absence of the loved object.

I envisioned this film as a series of dramatic tableaux historically set in the moment of photography's inception, when the medium was often conceptualized by poets (like Charles Baudelaire) and natural philosophers as the "pencil of nature." The film was to consist of scenes filmed in black-and-white with hand-tinting, where young man who, while declaiming an impassioned monologue, gazes at a framed photograph of a woman that he has never met (perhaps dead), and whose face is half-obscured by shadow. Veined throughout this story, the photographed woman herself moves in an almost somnambulistic state, as though responding to a mysterious summons. The two inhabit separate worlds that sometimes overlap through a series of spectral, ghostly encounters.

My use of characterization, dialogue, and mise-en-scene, alongside formal methods that I had used in previous films, enjamb one another in ways that suggest interference patterns rather than a redundant image of the characters' states of mind. My aim was not so much to represent a precise moment of photography's (or decadent literature's) historical setting, nor to present psychologically stable characters, but rather to challenge the very tropes of mimetic realism and historical "accuracy." I hoped to expose or reveal the ways that photographs—as sentimental keepsake and displays of psychological "evidence"—establish a scopic regime where women are excluded from desire and subjectivity themselves. More specifically, I wanted to investigate the question of an aging woman from the viewpoint of a desperate and disillusioned young man. What of the fate (and agency) of white, middle-aged femininity in the face of the voraciousness of youthful, heterosexual masculinities?

In 1998, I filmed many of the film's scenes in Buffalo, New York. At the same time, two intervening events shaped the course of the project: I received a Guggenheim Fellowship for "Radiant Eyes," and was hired to teach film history, theory, and production at the University of New Mexico's Department of Media Arts. Arriving in Albuquerque in January 1999, I met S.E. Hayward (now Eva Hayward), who was then a student in the departments of American Studies and Women's Studies at UNM, at work on an honors thesis entitled "Skin Trouble."

Nina Fonoroff and Eva Hayward

[Eva]: My thesis studied the representation of trans[s]exual[1] women in horror films such as *The Silence of the Lambs* (1991), *Dressed to Kill* (1980), *Mascara* (1987), *Sleepaway Camp* (1983), and *Psycho* (1960). My argument was that the "transmonster" (the transgender/transsexual who is "dressed to kill" in horror films) rips open the seamless structures of subjectivity, pointing to the social construction of sex, gender, and race. The transmonster destabilizes familiar ways that these identities have been represented. "It" (the transsubject is popularly constituted through this dehumanizing and indeterminate pronoun) must suffer the consequences of this transgression: to be eliminated, murdered, or destroyed by other means.

I explored an unorthodox prose style for academic writing, which interwove autobiographical accounts of my own transsexual identity[2] with the methods of formal and psychoanalytic film analysis. This approach was informed by my meditations on the indeterminacy of transitioning.

[Nina and Eva]: Following a series of conversations about our respective projects, we viewed a short excerpt of "Radiant Eyes" in progress, and started to consider the possibility of working together on a *coda* to an already difficult film. Despite her departures from conventional filmmaking methods and familiar psychological points of view, Nina recognized the indomitable limitations inherent in a film about a "man" and a "woman" and wished to layer its narrative into still more folds and involutions. From Eva's vantage, transgender theory—

---

[1] "Transexual Menace" intervened in the medicalized naming of transexuality by excising the second "s" in "transsexuality" both as a reclaiming of self-agency—a way of claiming agency in one's own surgical exploration of embodiment, but also as a critique of the ways medicine has diagnosed, pathologized, and otherwise articulated transnarratives.

[2] We wish to thank many "silent" collaborators whose efforts were indispensable to this process (however it may unfold). Chief among them are Michael Johnsen, Pelle, and Nico Candelaria.

beyond the "filthy workshops" of the horror genre and, more broadly, the constraints of conventional cinema—promised an intervention in the violently reductive oppositions of "man" and "woman." While she did not consider transgender theory a utopian alternative to these binaries, she nevertheless imagined "trans" as an acoustically-rich alternative to the earworm of popular gendered refrains. In the main, Nina agreed with Eva that these ideas posed an interesting challenge for her as a feminist experimental filmmaker; yet she remained ambivalent about how it all might metamorphose as sound/images in "Radiant Eyes" as it now stood. In any event, Eva agreed to participate as a co-writer and performer for the coda. She and Nina then began to work out how the section's setting and costuming could best evince their shared aspirations to mangle the conventions of "male" and "female" through Eva's then gender-ambiguous visage and voice.

Nina proposed to film Eva as a chimerical transwoman, luxuriating in a sumptuous sumptuous mise-en-scene, which included an assortment of textures, reflective substances, refractive and transparent objects. Eva would play a "witch," a powerful but somewhat disoriented sylph who might prove capable of conjuring a haunted, uncanny moment of transfiguration. The conceit was redolent of Gothic motifs, while also containing veiled and wished-for possibilities of a transgender aesthetics in film art.

In May of 2000, we filmed a scene, without sound, in the foothills of the Sandia Mountains outside of Albuquerque, using a Bolex 16mm camera, with both color and high-contrast black-and-white film stock. After viewing the footage, we were perplexed by the images' tendency to cling to an incipient masculinity in Eva's face that they had not anticipated: the layered percepts and affects of Eva's transition proved untranslatable to the camera's gaze.

We became co-scenarists in a number of planning and filming sessions for the coda of "Radiant Eyes"; Nina would solicit Eva's ideas about how she wanted the "trans witch" character to be represented, while selecting props, costumes, and settings that we believed could best articulate fantasmatic scenarios that would also attend to the well-being of Eva's sense of self in performing.

In December that year, we enlisted Eva's then-partner, Nico Candelaria, a professional makeup artist and fashion designer, to apply makeup that would exaggerate the feminine characteristics of Eva's face, to better meet the demands of a medium that was apparently resistant to the kind of subtle renderings we sought. Both the New Mexico and Santa Cruz filmings involved the "trans witch" enacting an orgiastically tactile ritual, wearing a long, sea-foam green, brocade dress (that Nina's mother had worn in the 1940s, and that Nina herself had occasionally worn in the 1970s). Eva caressed iridescent fabrics, beaded jewels, other glittering material, fragrant botanical forms, seawater, and metallic surfaces.

After reviewing all of this footage, Eva still expressed reservations about how the camera had recorded or "captured" her shifting gender expression. She was also becoming ill-at-ease at how her character's gender ambiguity was hemorrhaging into her own lived life. At the time, Eva was engaged in a more imminent change away from an interstitial gender that she had long identified with, to embodying a more "legible" kind of femaleness. All the footage, in her view, tended to bring up the painful feeling that the social dimensions of her transition might fail.

But Nina wondered if Eva was ill-at-ease because her stakes in the footage were shaped by her unique position as actor-as-spectator: the transitioning body as "trans witch." We both wondered about a spectator who would expect gender legibility at the level of narrative cinematic codes. These entanglements prompted us to seek out further ways to "rend the acetate": to find an epistemological break with the metaphysics of identification itself. Given the overdetermined quality of "man" and "woman" in visual representation from painting to cinema, we still imagined the possibility of bringing about a *sensuous transorientation* through film's formal devices, within the compass of films like "Radiant Eyes." How could this sensuous transorientation encompass many different kinds of "crossing": translation, transformation, and transfiguration?

For Nina, these questions compelled further thinking through filmic techniques and idioms. Histories of experimental or avant-garde films were already rife with challenges to dominant narrative expectations and binary gender representation, from Jack Smith's *Flaming Creatures* (1963) and *Normal Love* (1963) to Kenneth Anger's *Eaux d'Artifice* (1953) and others. Moreover, filmmakers like Maya Deren, Stan Brakhage, and numerous contemporary experimental filmmakers, even from a feminist standpoint, had produced incursions into mainstream cinema on many perceptual and affective levels. How might it be possible to combine formal experimentation (for example sound-image relationships using Eva's acoustically liminal speaking voice), layering of negative and positive images through optical printing, and a prodigious amount of reflective elements in the pro-filmic?

For Eva, it was a matter of lived necessity to try to imagine something that might be called a "transsubjectivity." How would the trans figure (or transfiguration) disrupt established cultural tropes or bring about an agitated awareness of what it might mean to be "trans"? She wished to mine these film aesthetics for their political potential, to explore the way experimental film might unspool oft-hidden ways sex and gender shape the way power relations, more broadly, are represented.

Speculative Digressions: Toward an "Irradiated" Body

Off camera and often *in absentia*, we continued to discuss, debate, and muse over some philosophical questions about the snarled labors while working together through our shared *and* differing commitments and perspectives. We wondered what avant-garde film aesthetics and transgender embodiments had to do with each other, if anything at all. Attending to this unwieldy question, we started by imagining scenarios where embodiment and sensation, working at the cusp of figuration and abstraction, could generate an "irradiated" address—one that would solicit both synaesthetic involvement and a "glistering gender aesthetic."

In her thinking about "irradiation," Eva drew upon her abiding interest in marine science and the physics of light to play upon *sparkle* and *glitter* as the building-blocks of life—"sequins as DNA sequences." In her mind, this was not merely a metaphor, but a means toward understanding light itself as medium and material—and also a way of resisting the notion of light as a universalizing transcendent force, as imagined by the conceits of Enlightenment philosophy. Eva also considered the ways that the light-sensitive materials of photography and film have been complicit in naturalizing the gendered surface of the body as a mirroring *reflection*.

Through these considerations, she turned to the trope of *refraction* (dioptics or "bent light") as a way to recast dominant paradigms of reflectivity that have defined the politics of film theory and its various posings of an irredeemably narcissistic subject.

For Nina's part, years earlier she had planned a film that would play upon the many textural, acoustic, and poetic motifs that were suggested by the Greek myth of Narcissus and Echo: inchoate notions that eventually found their way into the fractured narrative of "Radiant Eyes." *What could we do, together, to irradiate the narcissistic surfaces of both film's "body" and gender's "body"—to expose and refract the skullduggery of gender-as-surface and film-as-bodily-surface?* By using highly light reactive elements in the mise-en-scene with high-contrast film stock, we essayed different ways to "torch" the monumental edifice of film's historically unyielding projection of "man" and "woman."

We then envisioned (as opposed to its optical and lens-based predisposition toward representation *ad infinitum*) the materials of 16mm film as an absorbing and pliable surface. The substance of film—its silvered and dyed photosensitive coatings, and its acetate base—had long been, for Nina and other experimentalists, a resource for troubling the values of representation and excess. Specifically, to play with the polarities of film as optic and film as material membrane (sometimes within the same piece).

"Irradiation" became, for them, a figural device where light itself brought attention to film as material. In other words, while images generally reveal the indexical trace of light's relay, we conceived of "irradiating" this relay to amplify attention to light itself as the referent.

While teetering on the somewhat Gothic paradigms that had bewitched, bothered, and bewildered both Nina and Eva, we considered "Radiant Eyes" as we continued to investigate the sensuous address of "corporeal light" in this filmic encounter. We posited that the projection of "Radiant Eyes" might be charged with the expressive energies of filmic *substances* as they are framed by film's image field and sonic atmosphere. In other words, we wanted to increase the wattage of film's incandescent effect to the point where light becomes carnal, and its moving refractions have the ability to reach out and solicit bodies, making them *more* and *other*.

Further, the effect on the viewer of this onrush of pigment and color (the inks and dyes used in hand-painting film), contrast, and visual and acoustic layering is to unleash sensation into the bodily sensorium. Beyond the purely optical, our work would beam *into* and *onto* the body of the "viewer." At least, we conceived the trans witch as forming a "over-exposure"—by which we mean an excess of light that sidesteps the precisions of focused gender representations for something akin to a *transillumination* (passing strong light through the body)— against which the reductive meaning of representation and its various historical regimes could hyperlight gender's refulgent proliferation.

An Impasse

Nina was submerged in "Radiant Eyes" (now retitled "The Eye of the Mask"), which had grown to several thousand feet of 16mm film. Immersed in working and reworking hand-painted overlays on an optical printer; experimenting with "solarization" effects through superimposition of negative and positive images; fashioning the resulting footage into a loose narrative; and composing a dense sound design using hundreds of recorded sources, Nina developed the film's formal structure between 2000 and 2004. Because the synchronous sound she had recorded in 1998 (while shooting one of the film's major scenes) was unsatisfactory, she wrote and recorded narration for all three of the characters, using the voices of several friends.

Eva helped Nina to write the text for the portion of the film in which she appeared and recorded it in her own voice. At this time, Eva also saw parts of the rough cut, and continued to express doubts about the film's "readability."

While in the finishing stages, the film was beset by countless technical difficulties (mostly to do with lab work), which made screening the 16mm answer print impossible. The film premiered in a digital video format, under the title "The Eye of the Mask" at the New York Film Festival's "Views from the Avant-Garde" sidebar in October 2004. It was subsequently screened in a class at the University of Binghamton's Cinema Department later in October and at the "First Person Cinema" film series at the University of Colorado at Boulder in November.

At all these venues, the film's reception was marked by perplexity and confusion. The audiences' responses, as well as the nagging technical problems with the film print, contributed to Nina's decision not to distribute the film or seek additional screenings. She would go back into the piece and rework many of its sound elements, trying to reach greater narrative clarity and filmic resonance.

Answers to a Friend: Nina's Letter

In conversation, as Nina discussed with Eva her plans for finishing "The Eye of the Mask" (now languishing in an unfinished state); Eva wondered about the separate stakes for herself and for Nina. She asked Nina pertinent questions about

Your Camera Is Making My Life Difficult": Notes on a Troubled Collaboration

the relationship between the creative process of filmmaking and that of the theoretical musings that both women had undertaken years earlier. By way of an answer, Nina wrote:

Dear Eva, You recently asked me about my creative process; you also asked where I was to be found in "The Eye of the Mask"'s fantasy. While I can't promise to answer these questions directly, I'll do my best.

I am immediately reminded of why I dislike the term "strategy" when applied to the making of art, and especially films. Strategy—derived from military operations—implies that if an artist makes a particular choice at an opportune moment in the work's development, then a specific result will be netted. Artists' statements and theoretical treatises (on film especially) are also riddled with this canard, which neglects a knowledge that many artists, "experimental" or not, cannot deny: that it may not work that way. There is no correlation which says, "If I do this, then that will happen"; so there is no outcome that can be fairly anticipated, as we ourselves have been blindsided by many factors that have lain outside of our conscious control. Therefore, anything I can say about my "strategy" has been subsumed or enfolded into a process of uncertain becoming.

It's a commonplace that experimental filmmaking has no clear idea of its end result, and I remain uninterested in a process where one tries to eliminate all the unpredictable turns and byways. I want to surprise myself, but sometimes I fail to account for certain unpleasant shocks that may arise. Where there is unpredictability there is also the spectre of outright failure. I have to say that I'm now bewildered by what is happening to this film, and I'm struggling to remedy its shortcomings. After ten years of work on it, I also know that I'm too close to its images, sounds, its very molecular structure, to be able to see it in a disinterested way.

One serious challenge I undertook for "The Eye of the Mask" was to make a kind of narrative film without a script, and without actors who are conversant in improvisational techniques. So it wasn't simply a matter of working with a rough plan and setting up the conditions for improvised dialogue. I wanted to begin with no overall plan, no architecture, or outline, as I've done in my earlier films. The vagaries of this process, as I've said, continue to intrigue me despite its hazards. But when I work this way, I finally see that precision of meaning, especially around concepts that are as complex as those you have named in our conversations, is difficult to achieve. Nuance is everything; I must sidle up to meaning through innuendo and connotation, rather than by means of direct signification. I wanted passages of the film to reach a pitched feeling-state. At the same time, I'm not an accomplished enough, or perhaps generous enough storyteller to narrate in a voice other than my own, much less to build a contained fictive world, replete with all of the details and affects. The film remains autobiographical, with all the confusions, limbos, and ambivalences that that entails. In such a prolonged effort, moreover, I've given way to the unwieldy temptation to encumber—or, as I see it now, derail—the whole project by adding on extra limbs and segments as the years have worn on.

Here's a rough (not by any means exhaustive) list of what goes on in my mind when I'm editing a film:

-Which motifs to emphasize, and which to underplay?

-The minutiae of seeing one color against another.

-Shaping the movement, the moment-to-moment shifts in and between images.

-The structure of repetition: How much time/distance/perspective should elapse between the man, the woman, and the trans-woman?

-How can these optics achieve a felt minimization or maximization?

-The challenges of sound: working and thinking in a different register than moving in moving images.

-How to orchestrate the sound to demarcate one character from another?

Your Camera Is Making My Life Difficult": Notes on a Troubled Collaboration

-How to set a distinct mood or tone for each of the film's sections?

-How to manage the transitions between one section and another?

-What kind of narration can be reasonably placed within each movement—or within the transitions?

These are only a few considerations that come immediately to mind—there are many more. So, as you might imagine, the "formal" requirements of the film carry a burden of meaning equal to any consideration of framing the characters. Technical matters are never, for me, only technical. Like a poet, I have to pay attention to the minutiae of alliteration, line breaks, precision in the choice of words, and so much else in order to produce an affective world that is otherwise unyielding to articulation. In the film, I hoped to explore subjectivity itself; and, in my own filmic (as distinct from cinematic) language, to displace or disfigure familiar moves that have long been codes for characters' subjectivities in more conventional films.

Making films—the way I make them—generally involves over a dozen different machines, most of which I operate myself (I leave little to the lab or to other people). Only one of these machines is that conceptual device commonly called the "camera." In your personal experience of being "in front of" the camera, you have echoed others' animadversions: that the camera can become an instrument of violence and insult. Ironically, this is the very issue that I point to in the dramatic content of the "The Eye of the Mask." But what of the many other machines through which my material—and I myself— pass through, in uneasy relation, on the way to that elusive state called "completion"? The camera—and its projected result—are only the most readily comprehensible of all these machines to audiences and scholars. For me, the camera is by no means the only, or even the most important, apparatus I use when making my films. How can I uncouple my critical thoughts, my questions about "content," from myriad "technical aspects"?

Which brings me to the film's fantasy. But which fantasy, of so many? The film's fantasy is not singular any more than my own fantasies are. What seems most relevant now, as a political fantasy (not to say a place of intense personal grief), is what I have come to call my "federal case." As I've told you, I've tried to articulate this story, without success, in documentary form. An element of "The Eye of the Mask"'s raison d'ètre emerges from my critique of the male character. It has remained important for me to interrogate that man's usage of a photograph as a "stand in" for the absent, ideal woman of his fantasy. So, I have created a fiction of my own (nonetheless true, perhaps, for being a fiction) that this is the condition of a particular kind of heterosexual masculinity I've encountered. You could probably excavate this problem in psychoanalytic terms, whereas my perspective emerges from personal and anecdotal experience. It impinges upon my own sense (as we've thrashed out over the years over many a bottle of wine) that a "heterosexual" woman of advancing years—say, me, or the female character—must suffer searing losses and particular indignities, indeed a sense of hopelessness, at the hands of some man. Consequently, I have turned to the term "postwoman" to describe this state of traumatic resignation.

Yet, at the same time, I find myself in a conundrum. My criticism of the man's character, as I've depicted him in the film, is not unmixed with some admiration, even fascination or identification. It both amuses and alarms me to find the film's very substance sliding out from under my feet in this way. In another irony, I find myself in a fetishistic relationship to your filmed image, putting me in an uncomfortably close spiritual proximity to the male character. Does this betoken an inescapable tendency to "objectify" a subject? I had hoped to point to integration, or a "melding" of the male and female characters, using the image of your—a trans-person—as a cipher to wrap it all up, to "redeem" their tragic story. It now seems that I've fallen headlong into the very kind of utopian fantasy I wanted to avoid. I had no intention of making you a poster child for any part of my "federal case," either its diagnosis or its proposed remedy. As a welter of superimpositions, the film appears to be losing vital distinctions between its layers: it's turning out muddy, like a watercolor where too many hues have been placed on top of one another. These washes of pigment seem to have become—materially— like embalming fluid, and I regret this.

I lay all these matters bare because you have asked, and because I welcome the opportunity to think all of these "stuffs" through more clearly.

From a Friend and Colleague: Eva's letter

In 2005, Eva completed her Ph.D. and was hired as an Assistant Professor in the Department of Media Arts at UNM, making her Nina's department colleague as well as friend and collaborator. Meanwhile, Nina had removed the narration from the film's sound and still struggled with revisions to "The Eye of the Mask" (now the film's semi-permanent title), which languished in an unresolved state for the next two years. Then, in 2007, wishing to resolve problems and resume work on the project, Nina and Eva viewed it together. This was Eva's first viewing of any version of the film in its entirety. July 13, 2007:

Dear Nina, With some trepidation, I want to share with you my reflections after viewing "The Eye of the Mask." Please remember two things: 1) I deeply respect your work and our friendship; 2) The film that we saw can never be the film I remembered.

What I have to say tries to weave together thoughts about film analysis ("a reading") with something that we might call "negative" space . . . the space beyond the frame, and indeed beyond the film, that attends to us: me as transsexual, you as feminist filmmaker, us as friends and collaborators. To explain the troubles I am having with your film, I offer an account where "inside" and "outside" intersect: the filmic space and the vicissitudes of my transitioning self become stitched together. This is about how the film conflates my representation and embodiment experience. Consequently, I cannot write about your film, but only against it (as in propped or collided). I am simply too much a part of its physical and imaginary folds. To write about your film would be an exercise in evasion, because I, too, am complicit in my subjugation. It is from this standpoint that I share with you my thoughts.

Fragments from a remembered film:

The sound of running water

Arpeggiated musical chord.

A woman in a mask.

A man gazing at a photograph of the woman.

Hand-painting and crackling inks.

A shell-bowl, a glove, and a magnifying glass.

Another figure (both man and woman or neither) on the shore.

Blooming flowers and ripening fruits.

A woman ruined by a man.

A trans witch reveling in excess.

A man in bliss with the surface effects of a woman, but not with her herself.

Ethereal tones.

Extreme contrasts in black and white of tree bark.

High contrast Kodachrome color images of glitter.

A critical turn that I cannot follow through.

On the face of it, the film is obsessed with the effects of its own surface, layering itself with textures and luminosities. Although it makes visible its modes of annunciation at every turn, the film also appears driven to veil. This "I love the pieces of myself" calls to mind the fetishist, who disavows his castration and unconsciously shifts his erotic aim to some object so that he himself may remain intact. It is the film's preoccupation with fetishism and its conflation of the trans witch and the male character through matches on action and multiple parallelisms and shared motifs that troubles me. It is as if the film is asking the audience: Are gender ambiguous bodies, particularly trans women, fetishists who enact an objectification of women?

As such, I find myself, as a viewer, reading against my own identity. The film asks me: Do I desire becoming-woman through a negation of my material body, or parts of it? I get lost, even gored, in the film's calculus of inappropriate objects and desiring fantasies. Through this tangled knot of film stock, the film ensures that any reading of my body, my subjectivity, will always redound to maleness. The film seems to argue: If transsexuality is structured by fetishistic negation, then my own signifiers of femininity, my becoming woman, can only be construed as disavowal of maleness. Gender transitioning, the film supposes, can, therefore, only be a delusional act. An aside: this reading leads me to ask, where are you, the filmmaker, in all of this?

Among these fluttering questions and ruminations, I become lost in reading myself through and with the film'—as if I am pulling my body up from the editor's floor and splicing myself into the moving images and sounds.

Another critical turn that I leave in vernix.

What about the woman in this film? She slaps at the window of a house, at our view, at the camera's look from within the house. The woman seems to suffer an extraordinary loss, the tragic loss of being desired and then abandoned. She is Alice in The Looking Glass and he, the man in the film, is Jabberwock on the other side of the window frame, cooing and dazzling over her visage, her reflection. Is it too simple to suggest that this woman, this imaged woman, is not allowed into the house of representation? We know the now familiar idea that woman is never subject of desire, but only object—a well-worn though troubled notion. But here, in the film's fantasy, man/camera is once again in control of meaning. Why? Yet the Jabberwock, the JubJub Bird, the Frumious Bandersnatch are nonsense figures, monsters from dreams. Like them, the trans witch in this film is unnatural, a made-monster who dreams of changing sex. Is the man looking to become the woman? Does she desire to become him? And amidst all this longing, where is the trans witch? Monsters are fabulations, derived from Old French monstre, *from Latin* monstrum, *"divine portent" from* monere, *"warn." Can transsexuality—since trans women themselves can only be fetishist, as the film instructs—also be the object of dreaming for non-transsexuals, maybe even their fetishism? Are the man and the woman—as characters and as subjects— under siege by the whole jabberwocky, confronted by something unspeakable, or spoken only in nonsense: an inability to be real despite their patent desires and signifiers? Again, my questions crowd out my "reading."*

Here is where my autobiographical imperative gets the better of me, and I let it. The following lines are fragmented for reasons that escape me: Am I hurt? Do I simply not know? How much of my transsexuality is available to my own consciousness? My attempt in these passages is to offer an investigative web, a critical funiculus that both pursues and envelops. Perhaps I am most troubled by the trans figure in your film: my own representation. She is uncanny to me, literally un-home-like; a monster who became me, or who I became—in a wish to find myself as referent: the person who is represented. We called her a trans witch (sometimes "Ursule," sometimes "Princess," and finally "Eva"). This character caught me red-handed, so to speak, in my own becoming woman. Even now, writing to you, I cannot read her as "me," even as the film wrests a confession: she is me.

You wanted a gender ambiguous form to intervene in the narrative drive between the other characters who were playing out your "federal case." She/I was indeed their monstrous dream, their JubJub bird—a desperate animal that lives in a state of perpetual passion. The man becomes both master and mistress; the trans character (Eva) becomes man-as-woman. At moments the film seems to be a tale of a man who oscillates between desire and identification, so much so that he becomes the woman in an act of autogynephilia (love of oneself as a

*woman). Perhaps this was your intent, or perhaps not, I do not
know. But I do know that unfortunately, and painfully, I became
caught up in the goings-on of our trans witch. Through the
complex use of mise-en-abyme, the film structures within itself
a reflection of its own extra-filmic world. "Eva-I" and "Eva-her"
(the trans witch) became enmeshed together in the film's story;
"I" am precariously held in the prepositions of the film as both
actor and subject. It is as if your fictional film became, for me, a
documentary.*

*And so, picking up the stitches of my not self, I am struggling
with seeing my representation as not me, and yet about me. I
worry over the film's doubling and redoubling moves:
representing me as a gender-fluid fictional character while
using these image as documentary evidence of my transition. It
demands that as a viewer I see a failed self. I will never be
successful in "becoming woman": simply, I will never be real.*

*Looking at the skin of the film, I am confronted by the larger
wound of representationalism as associated with trans, the
absence of a wished-for referentiality: a real. I desperately want
to see myself as a woman, and I can't, or at least not as a fait
accompli. Corporeally, I know that my surface is just a skin. I
also know that transsexuality is a dense structure, involving a
network of hormonally altered systems, internal scars, libidinal
changes, cardiovascular diseases and cancers, and brittle
bones. Much of my transsexual narrative is unavailable to
vision, mine or anyone else's, even to my deepest
consciousness. And now, with your film, I am troubled by an
incessant return to my shallowly illuminated reflection, and the
utter loss it shows me. Does not the "trans witch's" figure--the
masculine shape of her face, the broadness of her shoulders,
the narrowness of her hips—appear as nothing less than
botched hope?*

*In "The Eye of the Mask," my transition remains an intractable
materialization of the loss of a referential sex I desire to
become, the loss of something I never had. "I will never entirely
secure my place as a 'woman,' "says the film, writ large. I
change myself in a necessary though incomplete effort to*

76

reclaim my sex, my fantasy of "Eva as woman, as female." I have sometimes described this as solidarity or "nearness to" woman, but this is sounds too superbly at peace. In honesty, I cannot describe this experience as anything but traumatic: I know I can't be, yet I am driven to try with undeterred need. So, I reach out toward my representation only to find myself (and it) cut. I experience a ripping open of my stitched-self, as the film ceaselessly drifts through narrative tellings. In the end, this is not only a violence, but also sadness.

In the end, the film leaves me in a snare: can my sense of loss be healed? The non-filmic me, imagines trans as a kind of regeneration. That is to wonder, How might my body lay down new collagen fibers, leaving a fortuna scar (tissue with a different texture and quality than the surrounding tissue)? Can loss become home-like? Can I make a body of my loss? These are the questions I wished your film, as you came to pursue a kind of filmic "truth" about trans, had helped me answer. Perhaps these questions exceed the scope of cinema altogether.

Love, Eva

It Takes Two to Tangle

After spending the better part of 2007 (-2013) "hemming and hawing," "fussing and fuming" in our separate spheres of doubt, we began again to discuss new directions for the film's checkered career. What could be salvaged from the wreckage? We agreed to split the "trans witch" coda off from the first 30 minutes of "The Eye of the Mask." (Nina now envisioned the longer film's completion under a different title, with its original focus on the tragic older woman.) The shorter film, on its own, was now a six-minute piece with narration written and voiced entirely by Eva. It would be reshaped into a more abstract portrait of an obscure trans figure who, moving along the beach, haunts it like a ghost. The title of this film, "Ursule," grew out of the conversations about the character herself.

Now, with over a decade of creative partnership behind us and numerous quixotic attempts at our feet, we still cannot definitively answer the question, "What were we thinking" and "what went wrong?" We can, however, provide a few cogitations that touch upon some things we've discovered.

Despite all our good faith efforts—full of curiosity, perplexity, occasional misery, and sometimes joy—our projects took on a life of their own, whose force and effect reached beyond the will of either one of us. No matter how we tried to predict outcomes or sort through problems, the material demanded its share in the work.

Even as we collaborated with and through machines and ideas, we were collaborated *upon* by these things, which shaped and reshaped us in our efforts to use them. The film itself proved capable of playing out its own mischief; and these oddities, seemingly animistic, cannot be easily sorted out.

In our attempts to manifest a trans sensual experience through portraying Eva's transition from male-to-female, we were even more convinced that our oxymoronic question for "material transubstantiation" through film is not exclusively about transpeople, but moves toward a more inclusive and extensive mode of bodily emergence for all those who engage film as a fully embodied encounter.

Our quest to *represent* the transwoman foundered on the failed logic of representation itself. Representationalism enacts re-tracing of some subjects' desperate desire to become "real" (*real* woman; *real* man: *real*). Our two (conflicting) agendas and desires—to represent—meant that at every turn we unknowingly stumbled on this irreducible obstacle, no matter how elaborate our separate choreographies of desire and hope. Representation itself is an ensorcellment for a real that cannot be achieved: soliciting and feeding on a desire that fixes it into "meanings" rather than a profuse field of sensation. In doing this, it enacts stasis rather than movement and force, and installs a staid past-ness rather than a vibrant engagement with spatio-temporal life. Through the logocentric demands of mimesis, our desire is rewritten into a demand for our own image, scraping representation across our skin until the abrasion leaves both film and self metaphorically and materially scabbed together. The film's luminous scars are also wounds made in "our" desire to *feel* the referent, the real. These grafted scars make up a tissue in which the literal and the figural are brought into contact.

Although our disappointed gender fantasies resonated with each other in scope and passion, our narratives required radically different forms, different affective equations, separate emotional stakes, and divergent lived lives. The tragedy of Nina's "federal case" was embedded within a system through which transsexuality is made invisible or dreamlike. She required Eva's lived gender fluidity (expressed through the "trans witch") for her narrative, in order to arbitrate the cruel nexus of "man and "woman." In stark contrast, Eva's "gender fluidity" was produced through an all-too-real embodied transition. Her performance shifted tenuously between fictive and real registers. Both our needs remained in paradox: our separate narratives were resistant to negotiation, while our wills strained to obstinately preserve communion. As our various film, video, and writing projects proliferated, our collaboration was driven toward its own inevitable unbinding through our incommensurable attempts at healing and representing.

In the process of discovering what did not work for us, Nina returned to an earlier and less narratively driven aesthetic, to dislodge the seemingly inevitable adhesion between the film's story and the thorny problems of representation—specifically, the trans-representation in "The Eye of the Mask." At the same time, Eva turned her attention to reinvigorating the critique of representation in favor of an ardent materialism of film, seeing materiality as an antidote to representation's toxicity, especially those of trans experiences.

All of this "toil and trouble," "sturm und drang," proved useful as a way to reformulate our understanding of experimental film's possibilities as a *percussive* force that sensuously envelops both the filmic body and the embodied audiences. As the film drums out its own materiality, viewers' bodies and the films' rhythmic force make contact as contrapuntal elements; an improvisation between the body of the film and that of the audience reaching into each other while folding onto themselves. Rather than reiterating the trappings of mimesis and identification, we in "Ursule" attempted to bring about a sensual alignment between the film's surface and the body's surface. This would be a mode of differentiation that can only happen through intimacy, the conjugation of body and film by way of the frame.

Like Edison's female creation "Hadaly" or Viktor Frankenstein's monster in Mary Shelley's novel—or, indeed, "the man" in Nina's film "The Eye of the Mask"—we were interested in a kind of incantatory physics that would enable us to *embrace* these fool-god's own perverse [acts of fetishization] luminosity the better to [build another perverse luminosity], to highlight and *irradiate* these follies of mimesis. In doing so, we offer *filmbodies* as a form of beingness, an ontology: not even epistemological, nor symbolic, nor representational, nor even spectatorial.

As Viktor Frankenstein's play with electricity to make a monster, Ursule was likewise a perverse being whose light play was witchcraft. A sea-witch up to no good with light, she used seawater to make light prismatic and substantive. Water ensorcels light: as light moves through water, it is distorted, refracted, and scattered. Ursule alerted participants in the process of making, performing, watching, and listening, light's capacity to make us *bodily* in ongoing and varying manifestations. Light's pulse, its irradiance, like a strand of DNA or a virus, is a living force that works like a contagion *on* and *through* our bodies. At the level of the atom, we are being altered by films' radiant index; we become luminous through our encounters with film. This lux-film form provides a denser understanding of the ways films can re-animate "spectators" as physical bodies, not as visual receptors but as physical agents that can themselves bring audiences into being.

The trans witch Ursule is conjurer of irradiance; she performs a double-move both as an inflamed gender representation and an iridescent technological device that further refracts the film's images. Her realm is at gender's surface, but weaving an extravagant plane of splendor and contention.

Ursule rose from the sea-foam of mimesis's collapse. In making "Ursule," we discovered that, as a medium, film falls short of "capturing" the many moving parts of gender-transitioning bodies. Cinema tends to be obsessed the surface of the body as a way of gendering its objects, eliding the nuances of gender. Although we attempted, through makeup and other means of mise-en-scene, to do a "better" job at representing transgender through Eva's character (the trans witch), it became increasingly clear that the search for accurate technologies of *similitude* was itself the problem, as these proved obdurate to the subtleties of transgender images that we sought. Nina's technical repertoire provided a way to "irradiate" the existing footage, layering and decomposing the image through hand painting, double exposure, and increasing contrast and density through compositing and optical printing. These gestures created a space for a transillumination to emerge, both as a critique of gender representation, and film's preoccupation gendering the body's surface.

From the Shipwreck: "Ursule" and its Progeny

While mimetic narrative films seem only to reproduce the same "elsewhere" everywhere, delving into film's materiality still seems to us a more generative direction that we need to continue to pursue in our differing creative *métiers*.

Working with "Cripple and the Starfish," a song by transgender musician Antony of Antony and the Johnsons,[3] Eva began exploring how to think about starfish limb regeneration as a trope for understanding the "healing act" of transsexual surgeries. That is:

---

[3] The name "Antony and the Johnsons" is a reference to Marsha P. Johnson, an African American transwoman who founded STAR (Street Transvestites Action Revolutionaries) in 1970 in New York. The group fought for food and housing for young, indigent trans-youth.

Your Camera Is Making My Life Difficult": Notes on a Troubled Collaboration

The cut is possibility. For some transsexual women, the cut is not so much an opening of the body, but a generative effort to pull the body back through itself in order to feel mending, to feel the growth of new margins. The cut is not just an action; the cut is part of the ongoing materialization by which a transsexual tentatively and mutably becomes. The cut cuts the meat (not primarily a visual operation for the embodied subject, but rather a proprioceptive one), and a space of psychical possibility is thereby created. From the first, a transsexual woman embodiment does not necessarily foreground a wish to "look like" or "look more like a woman" (i.e. passing)—though for some transwomen this may indeed be a wish (fulfilled or not). The point of view of the looker (those who might "read" her) is not the most important feature of transsubjectivity—the trans-woman wishes to be of her body, to "speak" from her body.[4]

As work on "Ursule" continued, Nina and Eva created several marine fantasies by applying dense media—nail polish, coriander seeds, salt—to 16mm and 35mm clear film strips, then creating moving images out of these strips. We imagined these as Ursule's oceanic dreamlife, which continued to exceed gender as well as human visuality.

---

[4] Eva Hayward, "Lessons from a Starfish," *Queering the Non/Human*, Noreen Giffney and Myra J Hird, eds. (Burlington VT: Ashgate, 2008), 72.

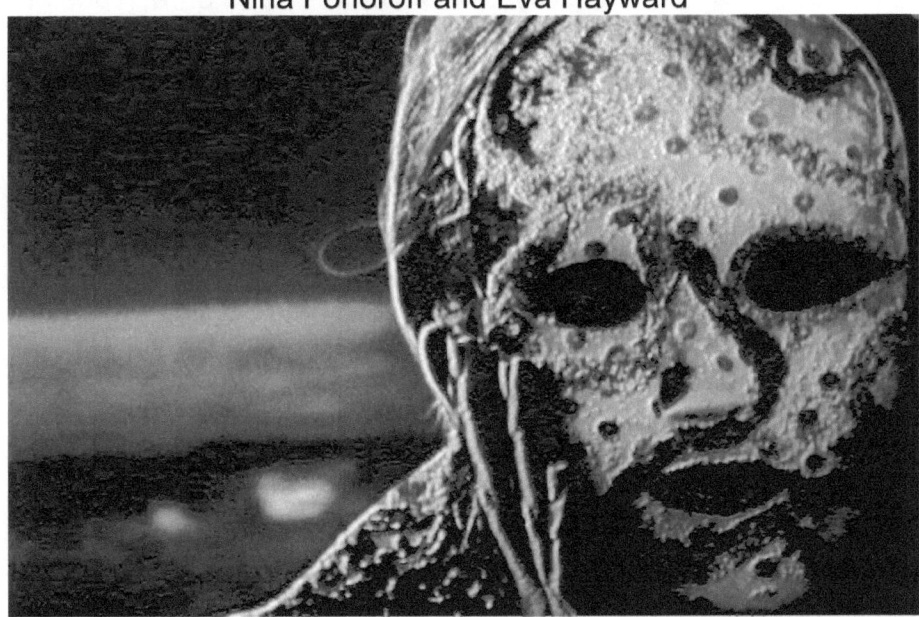

While pursuing "Ursule" and other film projects, Nina also jumped ship into artistic media that she hoped might provide more immediate gratification. Upon discovering that innumerable still images from both "The Eye of the Mask" and "Ursule" could be "harvested"—made into a viable, visually engaging set of pieces in their own right—she undertook various printing and collage experiments which combined images from these films with mixed media on paper. As she worked on reconfiguring digital prints, made mostly from a handful of film stills that comprised "Ursule," her friend, the New York painter Jackie Lipton, invited her to participate in a group exhibition entitled "No Regrets." The show would take place at the Westbeth Gallery in New York in April of 2013, marking Nina's first foray into the gallery world.

While she treasures the rich germination of ideas and exchanges that emerged from her years of work with Eva, the utility of this form of "deep diving" nevertheless remains an open question—at least where her work in film is concerned. Over the years of the collaboration, the entire process has variously affected her as a welcome distraction; a way of thinking through filmic problems; an inspiring proliferation of creative practices and intellectual inquiry; an opening toward a crucial (if painful) vulnerability; and an unremittingly frustrating and paralyzing endeavor. The title of the exhibition, "No Regrets," therefore arrives at an opportune time; it invites a look back as preparation for striking out in some direction forward. While there will be no tidy summation, Nina looks forward to irradiating other surfaces.

Watch "Ursule" online at: vimeo.com/158681611

Marcella Ernest

My 3,000 Word Interrogation of Racialization as a Visual Process

Marcella Ernest

As a Native woman who makes experimental films, one of my challenges is trying to talk to non-Native audiences, programmers, and curators about my work. I find myself struggling to engage with people in a meaningful way to articulate what my films are responding to, why they might be important, and why reimagining history is art. Our politics are not in the news and the framework for understanding Native imagery comes from American popular culture. So much of what we know about Native American people is learned through mainstream movies. In the following, I explore how "Indianness" and indigeneity are represented in American mainstream cinema. Drawing on literature theorizing the intersections of race and production of visual texts, I map the meanings encoded within the constructions of cinematic representation. I argue that the prevailing representations of Indianness sustain colonial discourse and practice, resulting in the erasure of the contemporary indigenous presence, specifically a female presence. Native American film is important because the oppressive simulations of Indian as stereotype must be reconfigured to afford new representations. Contemporary Native video art is broadly concerned with social power, redefining ways not only of seeing Native people but also of managing Native subjectivities and the ways tribal histories are talked about. I am writing about an inquiry into racial imagery, not racism. It is a theoretical interrogation of racialization as a visual process to show why film is such an important platform to challenge the prevailing representations of gender and Indianness that sustain colonial discourse and practice.

I use the foregrounded literature to narrate a relationship among historical image making, racialization, and Western imperialism to critique the power structures and visual technology mediating representations. I am thinking specifically about how Native American women exist as hypersexual stereotype in mainstream cinema. Informed by this literature and my experiences as an artist and spectator of experimental film, I argue for a more radical critique of Nation that challenges both dominant society's and Native people's perceptions of indigeneity in film and photography.[1]

Creating and Perpetuating the "Invented Savage"

In mainstream cinema, Native women exist within a male hierarchy. Scott Morgensen describes the colonial project as positioning their alleged sexual deviance as a sign of savagery.[2] With this in mind, the Hollywood Native woman's "nobility as a Princess and her savagery as a Squaw are defined in terms of her relationship with male figures.[3] In other words, the act of sexual deviance determines whether a woman is a Princess or a Squaw. In this heteronormative referent, indigenous social practices and sexualities are judged against a Eurocentric formation that determines what is "good" and what is "bad"—or rather, what is Princess and what is Squaw. For Native women in Hollywood, Indianness emerged in these well-defined representations of hypersexuality.

---

[1] While I employ "Native" for large-scale indigenous groupings, I acknowledge the distinct histories and multidimensional linguistic diversity of tribal communities in North America.

[2] Scott Lauria Morgensen, *Spaces between Us: Queer Settler Colonialism and Indigenous Decolonization* (Minneapolis: U of Minnesota, 2011).

[3] M. Elise Marubbio, *Killing the Indian Maiden: Images of Native American Women in Film* (Lexington, KY: U of Kentucky, 2006), 149. Referencing Rayna Green's findings in generations of popular music and literature: Green, "The Pocahontas Perplex: The Image of Indian Women in American Culture," *The Massachusetts Review*, Vol. 16, No. 4 (Autumn, 1975), 703,711.

Film studies scholar M. Elise Marubbio identifies the representation of Indianness in film as a "cultural iconography" that has been created and perpetuated by the character role in frontier cinema. The American psyche has embedded the Native American woman as a racialized and sexualized other. She is known as a conquerable body representing both the seductions and dangers of the frontier. To this end, cinema frames the Native female body as being colonized and suffering at the hands of manifest destiny and American expansionism.[4] Such mainstream representations of Indianness produce and sustain the racialization of indigenous women through visual signifiers that support colonial logics and practices, erasing the indigenous presence.

Media plays a crucial role in prolonging the colonialist legacy through what Ella Shohat and Robert Stam call "imperial cinema."[5] As an aesthetic of early films, cinema combined narrative and spectacle to tell the story of colonialism from the colonizer's perspective. In their critique of mainstream media, Shohat and Stam explain imperialism as Hollywood's Eurocentric aesthetic that produced this imperial cinema, creating images that sustain Eurocentric meanings of Indianness through colonial interpretations. These colonial interpretations can be recognized as absurd assumptions, threatening savages, sexually promiscuous "squaws," animalization, and other stereotypes. Colonial interpretations are also less direct and embedded in visual discourse of gender and empire. For example, up until 1960 the Hollywood Western genre was notably Eurocentric and famously invented the "Injuns" and the "Squaw" as wild savages.

Forged through narrative structure, these performances in Hollywood cinema were read as authentic and designed to sustain ideologies of conquest and savagery. Mainstream society's views of the period were fueled by "their interests in obtaining Indian lands and resources, a goal that motivated the

---

[4] Ibid.

[5] Ella Shohat and Robert Stam, *Unthinking Eurocentrism: Multiculturalism and the Media* (London: Routledge, 1994), 19.

public abasement of Indians, particularly in American popular culture."[6] Cinema emerged exactly at the point when enthusiasm for the imperial project was spreading beyond the elites into the popular strata, partly because of popular fictions and exhibitions.[7] Imperialism accompanied the nineteenth-century American expansionist beliefs that refer to a specific phase or form of colonialism when conquest of territory became a systematic search for markets and an expansionist exporting of capital. Thus, the theater acted as a space of modern power where the colonial ideologies of manifest destiny were seen and heard on the big screen in a strategic aesthetic framework. This framework repeatedly showed "wild Indians" threatening white society as colonial exhibition. Within the theater as a space of power, "the invented savage" performed as intruders on their own land. Importantly, it wasn't *how* the "adventures of savagism" played out, but rather that the violent acts and then the deaths of threatening Indian subjects could be seen, justifying the abduction of land and the necessity of their extermination.[8]

The invention of the tribes has been through theatrical performance.[9] Costuming, performance, and other visual and sonic signals are central to the analysis of Hollywood's representational strategies. Hollywood aesthetic was the imperial cinema archive of sonic and visual signifiers: war paint, war cries, war bonnets, and heavy drums are the invention of

---

[6] Beverly R Singer, *Wiping the War Paint off the Lens: Native American Film and Video* (Minneapolis: U of Minnesota, 2001), 15.

[7] Shohat and Stam, op cit, p 100.

[8] Gerald Robert Vizenor, *Manifest Manners: Narratives on Postindian Survivance* (Lincoln, Nebraska: U of Nebraska, 1999).

[9] For more on this conceptual theory of the "invention of the tribes" and representation, see Gerald Vizenor's work on simulations.

the savage. These films took the drama of the earlier silent era Westerns and added to it a more aggressive, bloodthirsty representation. "Wild Indians" are positioned as outcasts in what audiences understood as their Nation. The practice of "redface" —wigs, full costume, and bronze makeup—was an important aesthetic during this era commonly associated with the John Wayne "B Western." In Hollywood, "the status of a hero, and indirectly of an actor, was defined by the number of Indians he could kill."[10] The Western movie genre works as a paradigm to position living Indians as animal-like heathens who were induced "to perform a narrative of manifest destiny in which their role, ultimately, was to disappear."[11] Within this paradigm, the "myth of the frontier" and other expansionist fantasies had a central place in the American imaginary.

As a subgenre of the Western movie, revisionist films began to question the ideals and styles of the traditional Westerns. The revisionist films are noted for favoring "realism" over the popular romantic and savage portrayals of Native people. They also sympathetically included more roles for women. Marubbio examines oppression and themes of imperialism embedded within this genre by looking at representations of Native women. In the revisionist framework, she claims that women are assigned the "sacrificial role of the celluloid maiden."[12] Marubbio defines the celluloid maiden as a young Native woman who has situated herself with a white male hero, thus establishing the 1950s paradigm of "the Celluloid Indian Princess" who aligns herself with a European American colonizer and dies for that choice. In her analysis of the celluloid maiden, conquest and celebrations of white rhetoric and pro-white agendas position Native women to the margins of violence, leading to what she says is an "intense questioning on the part of many Americans of their national past and their imperial and neocolonial present."[13]

---

[10] Shohat and Stam, op cit, p 16.
[11] Singer, op cit, p 33.
[12] Marubbio, op cit, p 199.
[13] Ibid.

My 3,000 Word Interrogation of Racialization as a Visual Process

Still present in contemporary Hollywood, the Western narrative paradigm exists as a cinematic form of colonial exhibition. Filmmaker and scholar Beverly Singer writes that it is a general rule that Hollywood "Indian" movies are set in late nineteenth-century America. As a well-known example, a revisionist framework is seen in "Indian sympathy films" in productions like *Dances with Wolves* (1990) and *Pocahontas* (1995). Even in more current movies like *Twilight* (2008), *Avatar* (2009), and *The Revenant* (2015), the Western paradigm is still prevalent as aesthetic, perpetuating the ideologies of Indianness through savagery and violence. In hugely popular films such as these, "Hollywood Indians and stereotype contribute to the commodification and dehumanization of Native people."[14] What is at stake in these representations, even those that are "sympathetic," is the forging of identities.

A Normalizing Operation

Popular culture forged Native identities through simulations, prolonging colonial ideologies. Representations seen in imperial cinema produce forms of knowledge. Because "realism is theoretically impossible," the struggle for meaning matters. As a system of power, cinema has the ability to induce audiences with a discourse that creates a "fundamental misreading of American history."[15] Because of this production of knowledge, there are still truths in which communities are invested.

This brings me to a discussion of how Eurocentric films can construct normativities. An awareness of "the universalization of Eurocentric norms" is essential to comprehend media representations and contemporary subjectivities. Eurocentrism first emerged as a discursive rationale for colonialism, the process by which European powers reached positions of

---

[14] Singer, op cit, p 6.
[15] Shohat and Stam, op cit, p 180-82.

hegemony in much of the world.[16] Eurocentrism is not only a concept but also an indoctrination of biased perspectives, and Eurocentric/Western worldviews. These perspectives have become normalized and understood as truth through what Shohat and Stam call, "a normalizing operation."[17] This normalizing operation is perpetuated and established through a long history of film production. "Hollywoodcentrism" is the common term in film studies to connect the colonial ideologies of Eurocentrism with the industry of cinema.[18]

Because poststructuralist theory reminds us that we live and dwell within language and representation and have no direct access to the "real," films that represent marginalized cultures in realistic mode implicitly make factual claims.[19] Thus Native filmmakers are right to draw attention to "the complacent ignorance of Hollywood portrayals of Native Americans, to the cultural flattening which erases geographical and cultural difference" that collapse into a single stereotypical figure, the "instant Indian" with a war bonnet, long braids, and a breechcloth.[20]

Using mainstream cinema as paradigm, I have described a history of Native visual representations that is performed in American popular culture. This shows how mainstream media affirms U.S. colonial logics that disembody the Native and

---

[16] Ibid, 3.

[17] Ibid, 2.

[18] "Hollywoodcentric" is centered in a critique of cinema studies itself, claiming that cinema studies privileges "the West" and focuses on mainstream Western films that dominate world attention, but only make up a small percentage of the world cinema.

[19] Most of contemporary film theory is poststructuralist in orientation; poststructuralism is a position of critique that questions the rational methodologies and fixed definitions. It is the theoretical reconsideration of truths and hierarchies found within ideology and "common sense."

[20] Kerstin Knopf, *Decolonizing the Lens of Power: Indigenous Films in North America* (Amsterdam: Rodopi, 2008), 142. _____

renders them invisible and absent. In order to be a better spectator, creator, and appreciator of Native film, representation must be understood as important, first through a critical understanding of how mainstream society understands the Native subject by way of popular culture through a history of misrepresentation in film and ethnographic spectacle; that is the significance of this essay.

Visual Culture

In the following discussion, I map the ways in which I find visual culture an important site of critical analysis. I am thinking about the interventions that a critique of racialization through visual culture scholarship can offer to the analysis of indigeneity and further, what contributions it can make into the larger discussions of experimental film more broadly. As I chart the ways race has been taken up and expanded upon in visual culture, I further explore some of the discrete ways that visual logics construct knowledge, normativities, and subjects as "other."

Visual culture is an emerging field of scholarship that seeks to understand the meanings that images and photographic archives portray. Scholarship centered within visual cultural analysis is critical to unearthing and understanding the cultural and historical significance of image making. As visual cultural studies has evolved, Hal Foster famously argued for a shift in understanding historical and cultural contexts through vision as a social process. From this, the term "visuality" emerged as the scholarly understanding for images to be read as historicized and culturally specific. Expanding upon Foster's classic definition, Nicholas Mirzoeff posits "visuality" as a system of meaning that engages with culturally specific optics through historicized visual metaphor. Scholar Nicole R. Fleetwood argues that engaging with metaphor is a critical intervention to scholarship of non-normative projects. For Fleetwood, "Vision becomes a metaphor for the far-reaching arms of repression and the inescapability of racial markings."[21]

In discussing the study of visual archives and the colonial acts of image making, Coco Fusco, a Cuban-American artist and writer, observes that visual culture itself has been "an agency of oppression," calling for "a post-colonial investigation of the photographic archive." She writes that this analysis of racial rhetoric in visual culture, "Involves critical reflection about the implications of how the lines are drawn between art and propaganda; functionalism and beauty."[22] In this way, visual culture is a useful space through which race is posed and challenged, enabling film and visual scholarship to intervene in the ways that dominant society perpetuates stereotypes of Native women.

Another method of challenging the way race is posed can be found in the visual culture scholarship of Michelle Smith and her concept of the "counter-archive." Smith defines the counter-archive as scholarship and art that re-narrates a visual record's codification of racial information. The counter-archive thus creates a place "from which a counter-history can be imagined and narrated."[23] The act of redefining or rendering new meaning on a visual image can claim agency for marginalized subjects represented within the frame and because it challenges the structures of power by inserting a new dialogue, or new knowledge, with the world outside of the frame.

As Smith discovers the counter-archive in photography, popular culture scholar Kara Keeling explores the role of cinematic

---

[21] Nicole R. Fleetwood, *Troubling Vision: Performance, Visuality, and Blackness* (Chicago: U of Chicago, 2011), 17.

[22] Coco Fusco and Brian Wallis, *Only Skin Deep: Changing Visions of the American Self* (New York: International Center of Photography in Association with Harry N. Abrams, 2003).

[23] Shawn Michelle Smith, *Photography on the Color Line: W.E.B. Du Bois, Race, and Visual Culture* (Durham: Duke UP, 2004), 9.

images in the construction and maintenance of hegemonic conceptions. Keeling argues "common sense" to exist as "a collective set of memory-images" available for the memory to direct a perception onto cinema.[24] She uses Antonio Gramsci's "common sense" as her analysis to reframe what Stuart Hall famously termed "the problems of representation" by calling for a shift in thinking that will understand both "the black image" and "the white image" as inherently problematic, as opposed to "the black image" alone.[25] Keeling's "memory-images" include experiences and knowledge of the viewer that are available for the memory to direct a perception onto cinema. Like Smith, Keeling recognizes that a mental movement is involved in visual perception, and that this movement can become "habituated" or "common." In this way, she applies common sense as the condition of possibility "for the emergence of alternative knowledge." She claims that applying a new common sense to Gramsci is capable of creating a counter-hegemonic force.[26] As such, this complicates how identity becomes formed and, at times challenged, because it claims agency and offers new knowledge in a critique of the power structures that oppress people of color in mainstream media.

I argue that visual culture scholarship that centers race is essential to expand our analysis of metaphor in experimental films, found footage, archival films, and contemporary Native video arts as it allows for a much-needed discussion that is distinctly about histories of racialization through visual codes. Such a discussion is missing in film studies and film conversations more broadly. This conversation allows me, as a female experimental filmmaker, to address the formations of indigeneity and gendered identity representations in ways that illuminate how American concepts of these terms have also

---

[24] Kara Keeling, *The Witches Flight: The Cinematic, the Black Femme, and the Image of Common Sense* (Durham: Duke UP, 2007), 19.
[25] Ibid, 29.
[26] Ibid, 19.

shaped concepts of Indianness and how Native video art that is grounded in abstract metaphor can dismantle and recreate representations that are more in tune with the philosophies and expectations of tribal nations and communities. This conversation is also important to address how colonial representations of Indianness shape the ways that Americans and the rest of the world see and respond to Native people in movies.

It is important to note that I am writing about visual culture as an inquiry into racial imagery rather than racism. It is a theoretical interrogation of racialization as a visual process. As such, creating films that have the power to exhibit sight and sound in a meaningful way is an important platform to challenge the prevailing representations of gender and Indianness that sustain colonial discourse and practice. By thinking about the way people's thoughts are manipulated by visual perception, such an analysis is able to show how the gendered and racialized "other" is constructed as spectacle, how truths are created and maintained, how representations of marginalized people are regulated, how identities are prescribed, and it can expose how something like Indianness is codified.

In closing, Native experimental film is important to include in programing to support the project of reshaping identity because of the way that images can be rearticulated by a new frame of reference. Steven Luethhold contends: "When awareness of the dominant culture's negative attitudes is heightened, members of subcultures may attempt to assert their own cultural identity."[27] The struggle for control over the old images and toward new identifications occurs in experimental films through a process of visual repatriation. I ask you, what was the last "Indian movie" you saw, and how did you "see it"? This is an important question because how Indianness is performed and conceived matters.

---

[27] Steven Leuthold, *Indigenous Aesthetics: Native Art, Media, and Identity* (Austin: U of Texas, 1998), 23.

LOG HEAD HAS A HOG DEAL
LOG HEAD HAS A HOG DEAL
Maarit Suomi-Väänänen

Oh glade
had ogle
heal dog
ah ogled
had lego
god heal
dole hag
age hold

Nine years of work culminated in the completion of *Log Head* (2015, 10 min), the final film in the *Crazy May* trilogy. The two earlier parts of the trilogy are *Up And About Again* (2009, 9 min) and *In A Musty, Misty Thicket* (2012, 12 min). The common thread running through the trilogy consists of the psychological tensions, absurdities, and atavistic behavior portrayed in each piece. Throughout *Crazy May*, abandoned landscapes play central roles, speech is absent, inner worlds are exposed. A heightened awareness of one's solitude is experienced as we journey through the metaphors of life. The trilogy points towards the ultimate exploration of the inner state of human beings by combining black humor, cinematic special effects, and anthropomorphic beings. *A truly perfect celebration of madness.*

Explosions, smoke, stunts, special effects make-up, and prosthetics, along with artificial snow and blood, tell stories of otherness, depression, narcissism, alcoholism, and dysfunctional families. The explosions stand for unexpressed, helpless rage. If we cannot mourn, we might seek revenge instead. Whilst the soulscapes may be dark, I have chosen humor as my method. I see my films as experimental comedies. The works in this trilogy are many-layered and open to multiple interpretations. The narratives are open-ended and can be understood in various ways. My films invite the viewer to free-associate and be playful in discovering their own interpretations.

The reception of a work cannot be controlled; nor would I wish to do so. The genders and ages of the main characters remain deliberately undefined in each film. The central characters in the trilogy are a Datsun 100A, two badly behaved women, and a birch log. My works have been shown in hundreds of venues in forty different countries—in exhibitions, at biennials and festivals, on television and at various other arts events. Alternative spaces have included a parking garage, a punk club, a drive-in theater, an old folk's home, a medieval castle, the roof of a skyscraper, and several sports stadiums. My work has been shown in Canada more than any other country. These showings have netted two first prizes at the Festival du Nouveau Cinema in Montreal, and at the Toronto Urban Film Festival, judged by Guy Maddin.

The Film

Log Head is an experimental comedy about nature within us. *Log Head* takes an absurdist look at our dark side whilst asking where a human being ends and nature begins. *Log Head* is a surreal and psychoanalytical film about a human being experimenting with living as a tree. The synopsis of *Log Head*:

> *Log Head* is an experimental comedy about a birch log
>
> with a soul and a pair of skis.
>
> When Log Head is faced with the final chop, it takes to its skis.
>
> Will Log Head's escape be blocked?

The main character is a half-meter high birch log called Log Head. It moves around a snowy forest on red mini-skis with its lumberjack hat on its head. Its torso is sawn in half, and it has a gnarled crotch and a wound left by a chainsaw. Log Head has special skills: it moves, becomes moved, and moves others. Its soul is recognizable: it is envious of the handsome and wholesome Juniper. In an area of destroyed forest its heart breaks and it tries to unite with Stump. Log Head is sensual, and even temperamental: it gets angry when ignored, and in emotional turmoil it explodes, spurts out smoke, and changes color.

At the beginning of the film, Log Head runs away because it is afraid of being terminally split. The antennae and feelers of its emotions are the flaps and strings of its fur hat, which fly back when it is being pursued, spin around when it is excited, or droop when it is feeling disheartened. Finally, exhausted by the long journey and all the events of the day, Log Head finds itself by a river and takes a nap. The red mini-skis carry on shining red. The color red runs through the film—in Log Head's skis as well as some death cap mushrooms, explosions, and a river.

Log Head

I have been lucky enough to make all three films with the help of dedicated film professionals, all in accordance with my precise plans. The creation of the trilogy was made financially possible with funding from YLE Finnish Broadcasting Company, AVEK The Promotion Centre of Audiovisual Culture, Arts Promotion Centre Finland, and Finnish Cultural Foundation—a big thank you to all of you! Thanks are also due for artist residencies at The Banff Centre in Canada, AiRSandnes in Norway, as well as at Saari Residence maintained by Kone Foundation in Finland.

This is what the members of the core team said when I asked them, long after the filming had ended, what their personal feelings about Log Head were. Assistant director and editor Ville Väänänen, who operated Log Head: "Log Head could be a hybrid between a Teletubby and dwarf, with magic powers and the instincts of an animal." Cinematographer Sari Aaltonen: "It is a kitten, a child's imagination, the adventure stories of a grandfather." Special effects designer Konsta Mannerheimo: "Log Head is a survivor, a child running away, someone in need of help, but also a pervert, all at the same time. It has a wide emotional scale of sadness and hatred, and it is yearning to express its true self, but keeps being frustrated in its efforts." Sound designer Kyösti Väntänen: "Log Head is an individual and a person, just like anyone else, like any character in any

film. Impossible to figure out whether it is a man or a woman."
Stills photographer and camera assistant Jarkko Liikanen: "I
reckon Log Head is a guy moving into a city from the country,
so he is clueless about all the hassle around him, but in the end
he kind of finds peace, things might work out okay, a promise of
more to come." Yle Finnish Broadcasting New Kino producer
Sari Volanen: "Log Head is not old or young, man or woman,
not even a refugee. Log Head is just Log Head."

Fanny Malmberg wrote a piece for *Filmjournalen* entitled "Of
Nature, Humans and Human Nature" about *Crazy May*.
Malmberg saw Log Head as an orphan. I found her
interpretation very moving. Tens of thousands of Finnish
children were sent to safety in Sweden during the Second
World War. After the war, 55,000 found themselves fatherless.
In the last few months, more than 32,000 people have arrived
in Finland, running away from the horrors of war in Iraq, Syria,
and Afghanistan. Among those refugees have been many
children.

Children taken into state care are children abandoned within
their families. Log Head could also be the orphaned child inside
all of us. The pain is hidden.

Gender

So is Log Head a woman, a man, a boy, a girl, an animal, a
comic object, or just a birch log? I have already come across all
of those interpretations, and indeed, it was my intention to
portray a genderless, ageless, and neutral state of existing.
Sometimes Log Head is a child, sometimes an animal,
sometimes a man, sometimes a woman. Log Head's identity
encompasses both male and female characteristics. Could it
also be an androgyne, a third gender individual who does not
define of him- or herself as male or female? An androgyne
takes on whichever social gender seems most expedient at any
particular moment. Personally, I find dualistic gender divisions
insensitive, inflexible, oppressive, and depressing.

LOG HEAD HAS A HOG DEAL

According to the French psychoanalyst and philosopher Julia Kristeva, a subject is never constant; it remains divided and multi-layered. The true subject is always the subconscious subject. Kristeva is calling for a more critical attitude regarding one's identity. She maintains that our identities consist of both belonging to, and being outside of, the group in relation to which we attempt to define ourselves.

The Finnish language lacks a grammatical gender-specific personal pronoun for "he" or "she." Both are covered with the gender-neutral word "hän." The Swedish language is similar to English in this respect, but the Swedes have recently invented a gender-neutral personal pronoun, "hen," with the aim of helping to achieve not only gender equality but also gender neutrality. Every human being is permanently in a state of change. All of us carry our past within us—our wounds, dreams, experiences, and feelings. At the manuscript stage, Log Head was a petulant toddler as well as someone menopausal, and in the finished film it is also driven by its love hormones. The male menopause is discussed even less than the female one. One viewer felt that Log Head was a feminist free spirit, able to show its feelings and its desires, as well as its darker side of hatred, envy, and revenge.

Abjection, according to Julia Kristeva, is terror and loathing towards any philosophical entity that threatens to break down the boundary between The Ego and The Other, and between subject and object. Life-threatening abjection must be removed.

One viewer saw Log Head as a bachelor and a James Bond, out to find a woman, with his ego and his hormones riding high—in a spirit of magic realism though. Another said Log Head reminded him of his army days. A third one thought Log Head was an adolescent boy, and a fourth saw in Log Head the animation character SpongeBob SquarePants. A fifth thought of Log Lady, the lovable eccentric in *Twin Peaks*.

One might ask why so many of my films have something other than a human being in the main role. These have included—in addition to Log Head and the Datsun 100A—swans, ducks, a river, bottles, explosions, frogs, French fries, garbage cans, post boxes, as well as some less well-known celebrities instead of stars. When I watch a blockbuster movie, I often find my attention distracted by the glamorousness of the movie stars. Actors upstaging the films in which they appear?

The Forest

Research has shown that trees of certain species are capable of communicating with each other via a network of connected roots regarding matters such as nutrients and the shedding of leaves. Roots may join together even when there is plenty of space, as opposed to the Darwinian struggle for existence. This appears to be a manifestation of sharing-is-caring—not everything is based on competition after all. Some trees also communicate via the air, signaling to each other when to exude more tannin in order to prevent their leaves from being eaten. The part of a tree visible above ground is only one third of the total mass of it.

Log Head makes a stand for forests and for nature in general. When it is on the run in a forest, a beautiful virgin landscape of hills is visible on one side, but on the other, there are signs of intensive forestry. A clear-cut area there equates to genocide in Log Head's mind. *Log Head* can also act as a platform for dialogue regarding climate change and deforestation. In other words, *Log Head* is a film about the environment. The character of Log Head is a symbol of the spirit of the forest. Log Head is related to the goblins of traditional Finnish forest mythology. Finnish people have been referred to as people of the forest. More than 70% of the land in Finland is forest.

In this film, skiing is a metaphor for living, and trees have a spiritual presence.

Prop person Karin Pennanen, who operated Log Head:

> I remember my anthropologist father playing Father Christmas, with a birch bark mask on his face, a fur hat with earflaps on his head, and wearing a lambskin fur coat. This Father

LOG HEAD HAS A HOG DEAL

Christmas looked scary, definitely not a Coca Cola Santa. Log Head in the form of the spirit of the forest is searching for and longing for the last primeval forest, after all the forests have been cut down. Log Head, a homeless refugee, has drifted into living as a nomad. Even the spirit of the forest has been forced to wander around the earth. Log Head is rootless in many senses.

In the past silver birch bark was used for making bags, footwear, clothing, and food containers. We do not have a long tradition of urban culture yet, so in a sense we have only recently climbed down from the trees. It has also been said that without skis there would not be a Finland. In the past, many activities such as hunting, going to school, and going to war were only possible on skis during the winter. Skiing has also brought Finland glory and shame in the form of Olympic medals and doping scandals.

The forest is seen as both sacred and profane. The forest is where we go to make love and to die, to gather berries and mushrooms, and to hunt. Doctors in Finland send depressed people for walks in the forest. Exercise in the forest reduces symptoms of depression, diabetes, high blood pressure, obesity, stress, irritability, and anxiety. It also inspires a sense of community and an increase in generosity. Words connected with forests, trees, and skis appear in many expressions— including swear words—in the Finnish language. When things aren't going well you are said to be heading for a collision with a tree. Finnish ways of saying "fuck off" include "go ski into a spruce tree" and "go ski into a cunt"!

One particular scene in the film has attracted the most attention. This is where Log Head catches sight of a clear-cut tract of forest and attempts to unite with Stump. Log Head is longing for its lost family, parents, friendship, roots, its own missing piece. This desolate meeting place has been interpreted as mass murder, the apocalypse, and a battlefield. Log Head yearns for contact or even a warm hug. Whether Log Head will achieve what it wants—I have left that open as well.

Maarit Suomi-Väänänen

The Finnish poet Pentti Saarikoski hit the nail on the head when he wrote: "The forest is an academy, now destroyed by barbarians."

Premieres

The world premiere of *Log Head* took place in 2015 in Montreal, in the competition at the A Class Festival du Nouveau Cinema. Programmer Philippe Gajan says in the catalog:

> The return of our 2009 Silver Wolf winner (Up and About Again),
>
> the queen of anthropomorphism and of exciting and, shall we say, off-the-wall adventures.
>
> The third part of her trilogy leads us on the trail of a log with a mustache...

The front of Log Head's body resembles the female front in my opinion, but here it was viewed as a mustache. Nicolas Girard Deltruc, the artistic director of the Festival thought this:

> Union with Stump stands for union with the whole Universe. Log Head, having suffered much hardship, wanders around the now decimated forest, desperately searching for the right Stump, because it wants its DNA to live, and the forest to be returned to its living self. When Log Head finds the right Stump, it achieves union and ejaculates. The French word for a tree stump is 'souche', and the term stem cell is 'cellules souches'; both are able to replicate and renew themselves.

The European premiere of *Log Head* took place at IDFA 2015 (International Documentary Film Festival Amsterdam) in the ParaDocs series, the showcase for experimental documentaries and documentary experiments. I am pleased to report that this was my fourth time and sixth film at IDFA.

> In this mythological documentary about a human tree, experimental animator Maarit Suomi-Väänänen equips a little birch stump with a pair of

skis and a balaclava, and sends it gliding through a forest where others of its kind have just been felled. Wisps of smoke and mist suggest that the executioners have only just left, but the stump appears to have revenge on its mind. Skiing, falling and skiing on again, the little guy moves among the felled trees, sometimes pausing to ponder a particular stump. Is he shedding a tear? Is this perhaps a family member who has been brought down, or is he sad because of the inevitable fate he is facing himself? Groaning, he takes flight. Against the backdrop of this forest war zone, with the sound of chainsaws and explosions, we genuinely begin to wonder whether trees deserve more sympathy. Suomi-Väänänen creates the atmosphere of a cartoon film by using marionette animation and reversing the footage. A somewhat absurdist reflection on nature within us all.

In this catalog text, Log Head is seen wearing a balaclava, maybe even shedding a tear. Viewers had this to say after the sold-out IDFA show: "Thanks for challenging our ideas of the boundaries of documentary. *Log Head* is raising thoughts about what a documentary can be and endearing, absurd, and perplexing - a genuine work of surrealism!"

The year 2016 saw the Finnish premiere of *Log Head* at the DocPoint Helsinki Documentary Film Festival and the U.S. premiere at the Experiments in Cinema Festival in Albuquerque, New Mexico. YLE Finnish Broadcasting Company will be broadcasting *Log Head* nationwide.

Red

The film ends with Log Head, now red, arriving at a river and seeing something red flash by in the water. Log Head throws itself down on the ground, but is it to sunbathe, to take a nap, or to draw its last breath?

Personally, I see the red color in the flowing water as a reminder of the impermanence of everything. Neither joy nor sorrow last; karma is all that remains. The red karma of the explosion attaches itself to Log Head, just as our actions leave a mark, a stigma. The red color has been interpreted as a comment on the pollution of the environment, as well as blood and an echo of lost love. One viewer thought Log Head would be a more mature adult once it wakes up from its hangover. The film ends on a note of hope, with the last rays of the sun resting on Log Head. The end is both happy and sad; the old has gone, the new is here, but the plastic is staying.

Something old, something new, something borrowed, something red.

Allegorically, *Log Head* is about class divisions. Life is not fair. One becomes Log Head, another is free to grow whole as Juniper does, others are felled without so much as a by-your-leave. Must we accept this, or could we change things?

No trees were harmed in the making of this film.

The End

Maarit Suomi-Väänänen is an author, film director, media artist, artist filmmaker, screenwriter, video-maker and photographer, editor, producer, and woman from Finland. www.maaritsuomi.fi

A version of this article is published in *AVEK Magazine* (Finland) 1/2016.

Translation: Iiris Pursiainen

ARMed MANIFESTO
AGAINST RACISM AND MISOGYNY in Experimental Cinema

ARMed MANIFESTO
AGAINST RACISM AND MISOGYNY in Experimental Cinema

Kelly Gallagher

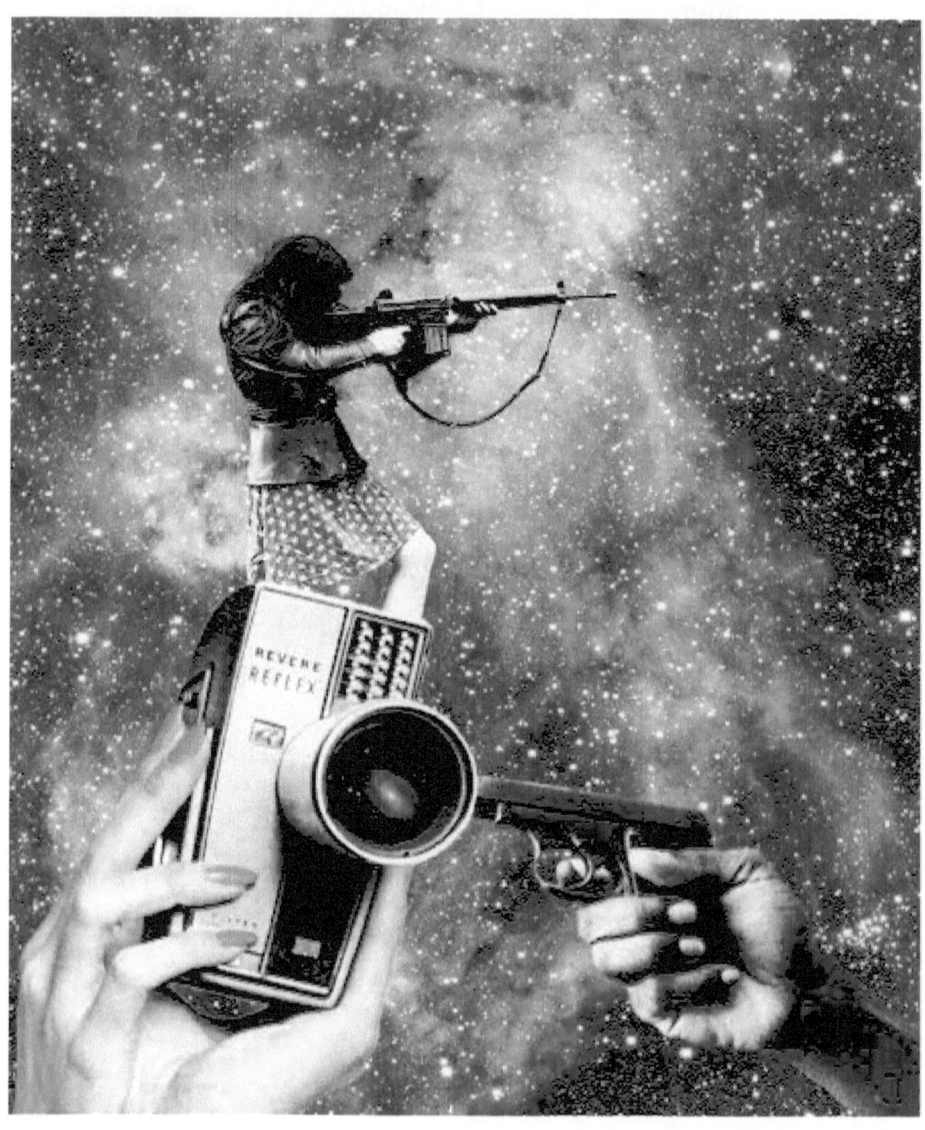

AGAINST: RACISM AND MISOGYNY IN ALL FORMS WITHIN THE EXPERIMENTAL FILM COMMUNITY

AGAINST: HISTORIES OF EXPERIMENTAL FILM THAT PROBLEMATICALLY EXCLUDE POC FILMMAKERS ENTIRELY AS WELL AS EXCLUDING MANY WOMEN AND QUEER FILMMAKERS

AGAINST: WHITE SUPREMACY PERPETUATED WITHIN THE EXPERIMENTAL FILM COMMUNITY

AGAINST: EXPERIMENTAL FILM CURATING THAT FEATURES ONLY CIS WHITE MEN FILMMAKERS

AGAINST: MEN AT EXPERIMENTAL FILM SCREENINGS GETTING UP AND ATTEMPTING TO COMMANDEER THE FILM PROJECTOR FROM WOMEN PROJECTIONISTS (YES THIS SHIT ACTUALLY HAPPENS, AND OFTEN)

AGAINST: WHITE MEN IN ACADEMIA PERPETUATING MORE SCHOLARSHIP ONLY AND SOLELY ON CIS WHITE MEN EXPERIMENTAL FILMMAKERS

AGAINST: THE CANON

FOR: DECOLONIZING EXPERIMENTAL FILM CURATING AND EXPERIMENTAL FILM HISTORY

FOR: EXHIBITING EXPERIMENTAL FILM IN PLACES OTHER THAN THE ACADEMY, GALLERY, AND FESTIVAL

FOR: EXPERIMENTAL FILM MADE MORE ACCESSIBLE TO VIEW FOR THE MASSES, IN THEIR COMMUNITIES

FOR: MORE RADICAL FILM CURATORS, MORE POC FILM CURATORS, MORE WOMEN FILM CURATORS, AND MORE QUEER FILM CURATORS

ARMed MANIFESTO

AGAINST RACISM AND MISOGYNY in Experimental Cinema

FOR: MORE WOMEN FILM PROJECTIONISTS

FOR: CREATING MORE ACCESS TO FILMMAKING EQUIPMENT

FOR: CREATING INCLUSIVE TEACHING SPACES FOR BEGINNER FILMMAKERS

FOR: MORE FILMS FOR REVOLUTION AND MORE FILMS THAT CONTRIBUTE TO BOTH THE ABOLITION OF CAPITALISM AND THE STRUGGLE AGAINST WHITE SUPREMACY

FOR: EXPLICITLY CALLING OUT RACISM AND SEXISM WHEN WE SEE IT IN THE EXPERIMENTAL FILM COMMUNITY

FOR: POC FILMMAKERS, WOMEN FILMMAKERS, AND QUEER FILMMAKERS SUPPORTING EACH OTHER WITHIN THE EXPERIMENTAL FILM COMMUNITY AND SUPPORTING EACH OTHER'S WORK

FOR: RADICAL CONTENT AND RADICAL FORM

This manifesto first organized and compiled by Kelly Gallagher with the assistance of feedback, suggestions, and edits from many filmmakers and comrades within the experimental film community.

Hedging My Bets
Bill Basquin

My scale of production is extremely intimate—usually just me or the addition of the person I am interviewing. That intimate scale is part of the fun in filmmaking for me; it is a kind of free fall—with the fear that falling implies, where the best option is to keep my eyes, ears, and heart open and see what happens. There are some aspects of that fear that are consequences of who I am in the world.

One of the members of my Advisory Committee in the Visual Arts department at the University of California, San Diego described his sense that there must be a rift a mile wide between who I am and what I engage in my films. What he was addressing, I think, is the curious position—outside of or in between, both or neither—that I inhabit as a female-bodied, masculine-looking, transgender-identified person who navigates spaces that might be easy to construe as hostile toward my gay body and my cultural affiliations.

By way of reassurance to people who inquired about the safeness of camping alone for a month in a forest inhabited by a range of wild carnivores, I said that the animals were likely to be afraid of me. What I had barely admitted even to myself—was in some ways unable to admit—is that I was more afraid of the people who might see me than I was of the wild carnivores who might smell me. From a distance, of course, I appear to be just another man alone in the woods enjoying "nature" and taking a break from his day-to-day reality. I am not able to reliably predict when and if that appearance will dissipate, but I sometimes do things even when I am afraid.

What is true of this research is that I care deeply about it. My imagination is vividly enraptured by the idea of an ecosystem that is whole—or that could be getting closer to whole, even if the wolves are heavily managed and half of them wear collars, even if "managed" means sometimes they are shot for "nuisance" behaviors, even if the successful repopulating of the species means that the Mexican Grey Wolf will be de-listed as an endangered species and, in some places, legally hunted. I don't like those things, and I don't agree with them, but they don't disabuse me of the joy of the possibility of this place I live becoming wilder.

I made six field research trips (April 2014, May 2014, October 2014, February 2015, March 2015, and July 2015) to western New Mexico. All of the trips were solo, and the trip in July 2015 was the longest at one month. Except while in transit to and from my research location, overnight accommodations were camping, which had the benefit of being cheap or free and of being local to the site of interest, enabling me to gather information and experience even in periods of rest or sleep.

As a Teaching Assistant at the University of California, San Diego during most of the research period, I had specific places to be on specific days of the week, and half of my research trips consisted of long weekends—thirteen hours of driving to get to New Mexico, two days there, and thirteen hours of driving to get back to San Diego. Because of these time constraints, I knew there was no chance for me to gain a broad familiarity with the whole of the Mexican Wolf Repopulation Area (which spans parts of Arizona and parts of New Mexico), and I quickly narrowed my focus to New Mexico and more specifically still to the environs of a particular stock pond in the Gila National Forest.

The wolves were what had brought me to that place and, though I wanted to see them, I knew that stumbling on a wolf's den site could cause stress or possibly worse for the wolves, so rather than looking for them, I tried to situate myself in a place where they might find me. To do this, I figured out what the wolves like to eat—elk—and then figured out what kind of habitat the elk like. I found a campground near a perennial water source that was next to a combination of forest and meadow, and I made that my base camp. The scat I found in the area told me I had chosen well; the tracks around my campsite said the wolves had found me.

I camped at the Apache Creek Forest Service campground the first night. I had gotten in late, maybe 11pm. It was April and very cold. I shined the headlights of the rental car onto where I thought I might pitch the tent and discovered under a nearby tree a thin, black garbage bag that contained the sawed-off forelegs of an elk. The legs were so recognizably animal and recently living; coupled with the plastic garbage bag—too small, not durable, and totally gratuitous—it seemed violent in a way that lingered and menaced.

Because the night had been so cold, I stopped at a lumber mill the next day on my way out of town to see if I could buy some off-cuts to use for firewood. The woman in the lumberyard office was kind, pointed me toward the pile I could take from, and said, "We give it away." Not far down the road into the forest, I began to understand why.

It turns out cutting trees for firewood, though necessitating a permit, is legal; the evidence of it was all over, and firewood was the last thing I needed to bring with me on that camping trip.

During a stop at the ranger station, I noticed an atmosphere strikingly different from the ranger stations in northern California. The place was not service-oriented toward hikers and backpackers, and the literature available was about a number of other uses of the land the places I frequent in northern California either don't include or don't advertise as such.

I am accustomed to the wilderness ethics of "leave no trace," "take nothing but memories, leave nothing but footprints," and "burn it where you buy it." Somewhere during that first trip to New Mexico, I landed in a very particular articulation of the word "wilderness"—not as habitat for everything non-human or as a place or a quality to be kept viable for people, but as something people use and manage to continue providing those resources.

I think of a forest as wilderness but in the language of the U.S. Department of the Interior, "forest" and "wilderness" have different meanings and different relationships to the possibility of resource extraction. The place where I was conducting my research was adjacent to land designated as "wilderness," but was itself classified as "forest," which allows for the harvesting of timber, the grazing of livestock, the hunting of ungulates as well as certain carnivores, and the operation of all-terrain vehicles.

While I was in New Mexico shooting this image,

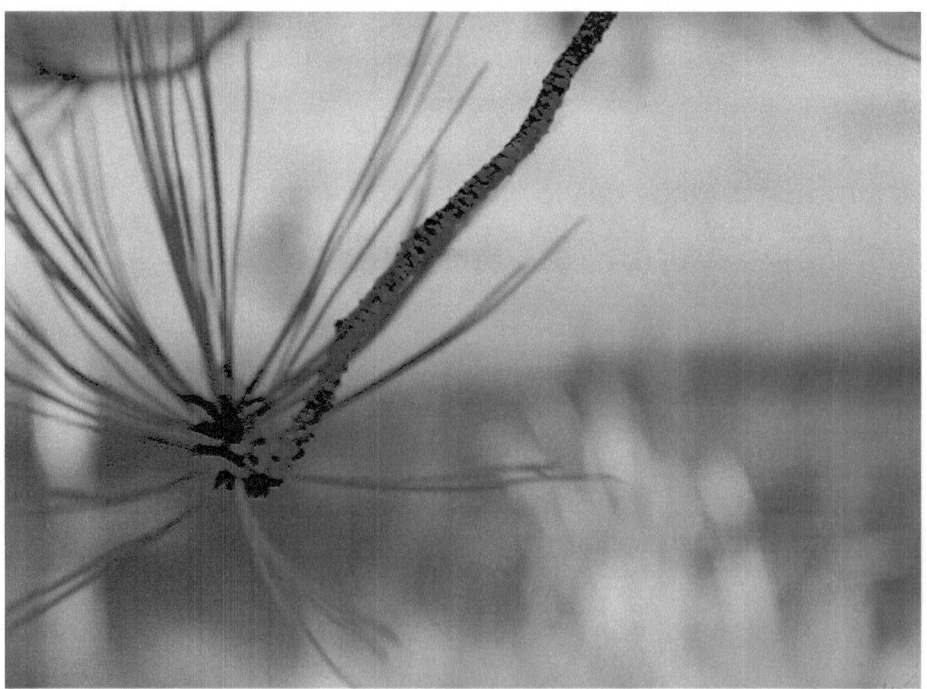

a man came up behind me and remarked on the size of my tripod. It was October, and in order to be very visible to the other humans in the area, I was wearing a lot of orange. The man asked if I was hunting.

I think this man was talking about elk hunting, but I imagined the possibility that he might be saying other things.

My projections of an alternate matrix onto the situation above hints at the potential of describing the space between who I am and where I am—the potential to both locate and dislocate my body.

I later realized that while hunters in Wisconsin wear orange in the woods during hunting season (at least they did when I lived there), hunters in the American West seem to wear camouflage. My appearance to the man in the forest must not have been one of "hunterliness," but perhaps one of indeterminateness or mistaken identity—of someone using seemingly related codes, but in the wrong way, to produce confusion and error rather than clarity.

On the first night of the month-long July research trip, my usual spot was already occupied when I drove in after dark, and I picked a site down the road a little near a clump of trees at the mouth of a canyon where I had seen others camp the previous autumn during elk hunting season. I pitched my one-person tent rather than setting up the big tent in the hopes that I would be able to move to my regular site the following day.

I never like making camp after dark. That's less about the difficulty of setting up the tent without general ambient light than it is that being able to survey the area in daylight makes me feel safer.

But I had no trouble falling asleep, and I didn't wake until the next morning—still dark out when the birds began to sing. I was lying on my back in a tent barely tall enough to sit up when I became aware of footsteps that, although quiet, seemed to be coming from an animal that was large. The next thing I heard was a deep, loud purr next to the door of my tent.

Hedging My Bets

I can be disdainful of human fear of wild predators as an explanation for human violence against them—partly because I am very experienced at camping in wilderness areas and partly because I have the luxury of living in denial. Once the sun had risen and I had mostly recovered from the adrenaline of hearing a mountain lion outside my tent, I felt that fear was the perfect introduction to a month spent alone in the woods—that the fear got me in closer proximity to some of my fellow humans (past and present) whose material and historical circumstances would have put them into more regular and less voluntary contact with mountain lions, wolves, and bears.

Later in July, when I was driving on the road near sunset, I saw a wolf. The animal was probably a young adult who was dispersing from its birth family and looking for a mate. This is considered the most dangerous time for wolves because in order to find a mate and a territory to share with that mate, they become vulnerable to the defensive violence that may result from their traversing the territories of others.

I am more used to working with livestock than with wildlife, but I know about the concept of flight zones—a kind of space cushion necessary to leave between oneself and an animal in order not to pressure them into flight. Once I saw the wolf, I stopped. I didn't want to pressure it; nor did I want to encourage it to come closer to me. Habituation to humans is sure death to a wolf.

This animal, whom I later learned was probably male, saw me, got a safe distance away, and then turned around and watched me. I think of this as prey behavior. And from it, I extrapolated that wolves, who are apex predators and seem to be among those in the food chain with the most power, are also constantly vigilant, constantly afraid, constantly making adjustments and decisions in order to increase their chances to survive or thrive.

The material produced by my filmmaking methods is a function of my specificity—of my discrete embodiedness. The film that I am making about my research in the Mexican Wolf

Bill Basquin

Repopulation Area is a work-in-progress and what is most explicitly in-process, now is my thinking about what I encountered and how my gender—its liquidity, perhaps, the way in which it affords me a certain kind of privilege and certainly a way in which it enables me to hedge by bets against my own fear—is an inextricable part of my investigation into fractured ecosystems.

Artist's Statement

Elizabeth Sher

Background

Elizabeth Sher is an artist and filmmaker working in the San Francisco Bay Area, where she is owner of I.V. Studios: Art and Film for the 21st Century. She is Professor Emeritus of Art at the California College of the Arts in San Francisco and Oakland, where she taught Painting and Media Arts for more than thirty years.

Sher is the winner of the 2014 Fleishhacker Small Film Grant and the 2012 Roy Dean Grant for Film. The documentary *PENNY* © 2014, directed by Sher, won Audience Favorite at Mill Valley Film Festival, CA and First Place at Intendence Film Festival in Denver, CO. *PENNY* was an Official Selection at Big Muddy Film Festival, MI; Athens International Film Festival, OH: Rochester Film Festival, NY; OUTrageous Film Festival, Santa Barbara, CA; and Port Townsend Film Festival, WA.

Sher's artist books, prints, and paintings have been exhibited at many university art museums and are included in the collections of the San Francisco Museum of Art, Fine Arts Museum of California, San Jose Museums of Art, Oakland Museum of Art, the Carnegie Mellon University Hunt Collection, and the United States Embassy Collection. She has had solo exhibitions in the San Francisco Bay Area and nationally.

Statement

Throughout my career, I have pursued a personal journey. My first film, *The Training* © 1979, was a satire on the behavior modification technique of toilet training, made while my son was "in process." I had never made a film before: doing so freed me from the constraints of my patriarchal art education—the Rules—and opened up my practice to the power of humor. When I screened the film, audiences laughed; finally, here was tangible success! I knew my work had reached its target–a laugh is undeniable. I was hooked.

Many of my films have taken the form of documentaries and quirky shorts focusing on women, art, and healthy aging, following my own life as a wife, mother/grandmother, and artist; examples include: *Too Young to Date; Celluloid Seduction; Stalls; Approaching the 14th Moon (women and health professionals discuss menopause); Younger, Thinner, Smoother*, and *Bella Bella*. Throughout my college and graduate school education, I never once had a female professor or mentor, and like many women of my generation, I experienced both overt and covert sexism when I strove to achieve. My Program Chair called me "an ax-wielding woman" in my tenure review—strong women need not apply!

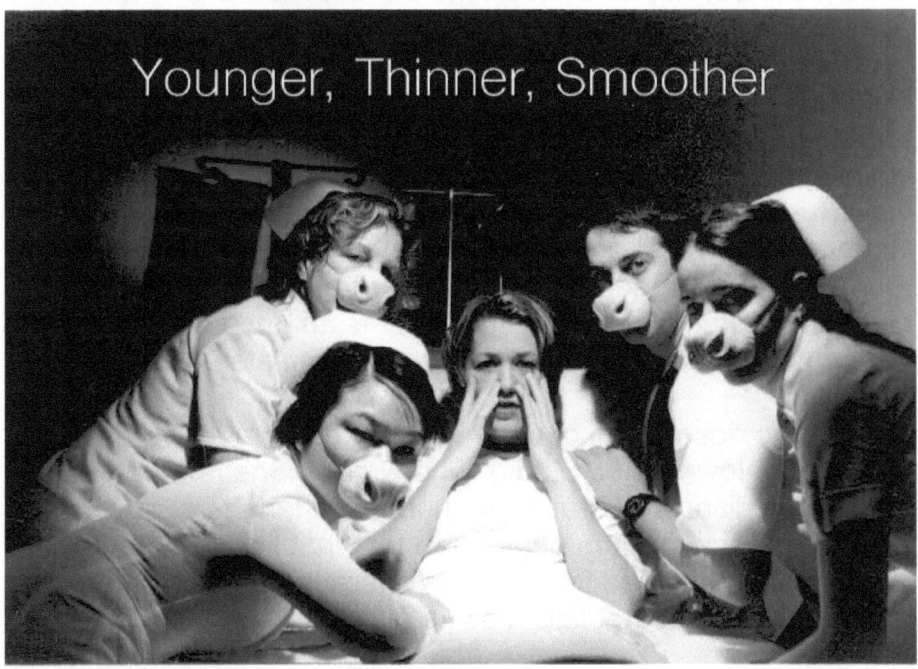

My 2014 documentary film *PENNY* follows the life of Penny Cooper, who faced similar challenges. Penny's nationally famous torts professor at Boalt (now Berkeley) Law School publicly opined that women had no place in the law school at all. Now in her seventies, Penny is a brilliant, funny, and successful criminal trial attorney, social activist, a lesbian, and an incredible role model. She and her wife, poet Rena Rosenwasser, have one of the largest collections in the country of art by women. Penny overcame the challenges of anti-Semitism, sexism, and gender discrimination, all the while keeping both her sense of purpose and her sense of humor. She is a beacon of light for all women (and men) who aspire to be the next generation of groundbreakers.

In my own practice spanning various mediums, I take inspiration from figures like Bruce Conner, Lynn Hershman Leeson, and William Kentridge—artists who pass freely between static and moving images, paint and pixels, traditional and new media. Conceptually speaking, all of my work is essentially developed through the same process: a series of edits—what I like to call interruptions, interceptions, and interventions. But it's also fun/ny: as Freud wrote, "Humor is not resigned, it is rebellious." I use irony and humor to thread together narratives of everyday life and its small absurdities, while at the same time giving voice to my own inner life and its vicissitudes. I try to make connections with the viewer both visually and psychologically: though I provide a map for their journey, I leave space for each viewer to find his or her own clues and perceptions. The final work is an encounter waiting to happen; the response of the audience completes the work.

My favorite description of what I do comes from Kay Flavell, director of New Pacific Studio, who writes: "Sher's vision of the human condition celebrates our humanity, laughs at our absurdities, and honors our search for what lies between our present and imagined frontiers. By liberating herself, Sher has arrived at a vision that liberates us all."

FILMOGRAPHY

In Progress - "Rituals of Remembrance" written, produced, and directed with Maggie Simpson Adams, 30 min.

Elizabeth Sher

"Penny," 2014, 30 min documentary written, produced, and directed by Elizabeth Sher.

"Video Sketches – Iceland," 2012.
- *Learning Icelandic Pronunciation by Elizabeth Sher*, 3 min.
- *Wind and Water*, 3 min.
- *Tractor Rap*, 2:30 min.
- *Baking Hverbroadt*, 3 min.
- *Slow Flow* (produced with Brooke Holve), 3 min.

"Bella Bella," 2007, 26:40 min documentary written, produced, directed by Elizabeth Sher.

"Stalls," 2004, 3 min mock-instructional video made with Maggie Simpson.

"Alma's Jazzy Marriage," 2004, 26:40 min documentary made with Mal and Sandra Sharpe

"Younger, Thinner, Smoother," 2000, 51 min documentary produced, directed, and edited by Elizabeth Sher.

"Chimera House," 1998, independent feature film produced by Elizabeth Sher. Story by Elizabeth Sher and Brandy Brawner. Directed by Brandy Brawner.

"Men are from Moon," 1998, videotape documentary short, conceived, produced, and edited by Elizabeth Sher, 5 min,

"Homenaje a Tenochtitlán - An Installation for Day of the Dead," installation by Carmen Lomas Garza, 1997, 24 min. videotape documentary, directed and edited by Elizabeth Sher.

"When Women Go Through Menopause, Where Do Men Go?" 1996, 56:30 min videotape documentary, conceived, produced, and edited by Elizabeth Sher.

"The Master-Mentor Series" 3-part documentary series with master artists/professors at the California College of Arts and Crafts. 1995, videotapes conceived, produced, and edited by Elizabeth Sher, 18 minutes each.

"Fingers That Tickle and Delight," an interview with deaf humorist Evelyn Zola, 1994, videotape conceived, produced, and edited by Elizabeth Sher, interpreted by Sharon Neumann Solow, 32 min.

"Approaching the 14th Moon" women and health professionals discuss menopause, 1993,

videotape documentary conceived, produced, and edited by
Elizabeth Sher, 52 min.

"Show 'n Tell Stories" 1993 Series 1, videotaped stories for
deaf toddlers in ASL and SEE

"Languages," 21 min., introduction by Marlee Matlin., for C.E.I.D.,
produced and directed by Elizabeth Sher.

"Fight the Bull," 1992, PSA conceived, produced, and edited by
Elizabeth Sher, 4 min.

"Celluloid Seduction," 1991, videotape conceived, produced,
directed, and edited by Elizabeth Sher.

"Just Another Weekend," 1989, independent debut feature film.
Producer, Director, and Editor.

"I. V. Magazine," independently produced magazine format, annual
1 hour annual program produced, directed, edited, and
conceived by Elizabeth Sher - 1986, 1985, 1984

"The Library Series" videotaped interviews conceived, produced,
directed, and edited by Elizabeth Sher.

- "Women by Women" - Chicano artists discuss their work
  at Galleria de la Raza, S.F. 1984
- "Dancing on the Edge of Success" an interview with
  dancer Margaret Jenkins 1988
- "How to Market a Body of Art" commissioned by the
  Union of Independent College of Art, for art college
  undergraduates, 1984.
- "Interviews with Artists" Programs 1, 2, 3, and 4 1988 -
  1994.

"Juggling," 16mm film, 1981, 14 min., color, sound.
"Too Young to Date," 16mm film, 1980, 4 min., color, sound.
"Wash It," 16mm film, 1980, 6 min., color, sound.
"Beat It," 16mm film, 1980, 5 min., color, sound.
"The Training," 16mm film, 1979, 9 min., b/w, sound.

Selected work on films/videos of other independent film/video
artists:

"Dancing From the Inside Out" video documentary by Sarah
Shockley, cinematographer

Elizabeth Sher
"Adam Hakeem - One Who Survived" video documentary by
Thalia Drori, post production supervisor
"Emerald Cities" independent feature film by Rick Schmidt,
cinematographer
"Citizen" independent feature film by William Farley, additional
editing
"Alone in the Tee Shirt Zone" independent feature film by Mikel
Anderson and Kathleen Beeler, additional editing
"Man in the Streets Productions" independent broadcast video
show by Mal Sharpe, Editor

For further information, images, and videos, please visit the
web links below:

www.ivstudios.com
www.pennythedocumentary.com

This yearbook is supported by generous funding from the British Council/Arts Council of the England Artists' International Development Fund scheme, AV-arkki Distribution Centre for Finnish Media Art, AVEK Promotion Centre for Audiovisual Culture, Finnish Cultural Foundation, New Mexico Humanities Council, New Mexico Arts, McCune Charitable Foundation, and Albuquerque Community Foundation's FUNd program.

www.ingramcontent.com/pod-product-compliance
Lightning Source LLC
Chambersburg PA
CBHW022003170526
45157CB00003B/1115